HIDING MY CANDY

THE LADY CHABLIS

THE AUTOBIOGRAPHY OF

HIDING MY CANDY

THE GRAND EMPRESS OF SAVANNAH

THE LADY CHABLIS

WITH THEODORE BOULOUKOS

INTRODUCTION BY JOHN BERENDT
ORIGINAL PHOTOGRAPHY BY ROBIN BOWMAN

POCKET BOOKS
NEW YORK • LONDON • TORONTO • SYDNEY • TOKYO • SINGAPORE

POCKET BOOKS, A DIVISION OF SIMON & SCHUSTER INC.
1230 AVENUE OF THE AMERICAS, NEW YORK, NY 10020

COPYRIGHT © 1996 BY THE LADY CHABLIS
INTRODUCTION COPYRIGHT © 1996 BY JOHN BERENDT
ORIGINAL PHOTOGRAPHY COPYRIGHT © BY ROBIN BOWMAN
INTERIOR DESIGN BY ELIZABETH VAN ITALLIE

LIBRARY OF CONGRESS CATALOGING-IN-PUBLICATION DATA

LADY CHABLIS, 1957–
HIDING MY CANDY: THE AUTOBIOGRAPHY OF THE GRAND EMPRESS OF
SAVANNAH / BY THE LADY CHABLIS ; WITH THEODORE BOULOUKOS.
P. CM.
ISBN 0-671-52094-6
1. LADY CHABLIS, 1957– 2. FEMALE IMPERSONATORS—UNITED
STATES—BIOGRAPHY. 3. TRANSVESTITES—UNITED STATES—BIOGRAPHY.
I. BOULOUKOS, THEODORE. II. TITLE.
PN2287.L14A3 1996
792.7'028'092—DC20
[B]
96-11046
CIP

FIRST POCKET BOOKS HARDCOVER PRINTING AUGUST 1996
10 9 8 7 6 5 4 3 2 1
POCKET AND COLOPHON ARE REGISTERED TRADEMARKS OF
SIMON & SCHUSTER INC.
PRINTED IN THE U.S.A.

FOR AUNT KATIE BELL (1936–1996),
WHO TAUGHT ME ABOUT LIFE,
AND MISS TINA DEVORE, WHO SHOWED ME
HOW TO LIVE IT.

A C K N O W L

UNTIL I DECIDED to write my life story, I never once had a moment to slow down and consider why my life had brought me to one point or another. I just kept going—it's what I know best, besides being The Lady. Though I've always envisioned success as part of my future, the love and support that have met me through this project have surpassed my greatest imagining.

I'm deeply indebted to my family—both of them. Some members you will come to know in the pages to follow, others I have saved for myself. I wish to thank my brilliant editor at Pocket Books, Sue Carswell, whose idea it was to commit my life story to print. She's also responsible for finding my collaborator, Ted Bouloukos, whose quick-witted intelligence and detailed devotion to the rendering of my life never once wavered during our year-long association. Much obliged, Ted. My initial line editor, Sarah Pettit, used her careful eye to trim this manuscript into *Hiding My Candy*. All right, girl! Thanks to others at Pocket Books, including my publisher, Gina Centrello, my associate publisher, Kara Welsh, and Craig Hillman. My gratitude goes out to all of you. Next time, "Uncle" Bill Grose, dinner's on me! And as for you, Robin Bowman, here's hoping all the world will see me through your eyes.

Thanks to David Hutchings, a former reporter at *People*

EDGMENTS

magazine, whose interest in my story attracted Pocket Books.

Of course, I wouldn't be anywhere without my transportation, Mr. John Berendt, whose successful *Midnight in the Garden of Good and Evil* has sent me careening into whole new worlds. Thank you, Mr. Limo Driver.

I'm deeply indebted to the following friends: Tim, Michael, Bill, Dehn, Li'l Jim, Linda, Keith, Sam, Chevon, Robin, Shaun, Russ, and The Savannah Production Group. To John and Thomas, my traveling roots. To Danny, the first man to put me in fur. To David, my manager and friend, to Dawn, my friend and fashion designer, you are my hands and feet, I would be lost without you. To Aunt Kate, from the nipple to your last few dollars, thank you. And special thanks to my angel, James.

Thanks to the infamous Club One and to all the crazy bitches in the show's cast, to Miss Mary and to Jeff, my liaison to the fans, and to Cale for providing the silver lining.

Last, but certainly not least, I wish to thank the protectors of The Doll's new fortune: my agent at ICM, Sloan Harris, and my lady lawyer, Kathleen Aderhold, who both covered for The Doll's ass on the *official* front.

Okay, that's enough of y'all.

— THE LADY

CONTENTS

MURDER, HE WROTE—SAVANNAH'S MERCER HOUSE.
THE SCENE OF THE CRIME IN JOHN BERENDT'S
MIDNIGHT IN THE GARDEN OF GOOD AND EVIL.

"You did then what
you knew how to do.
When you knew better
you did better."
—Maya Angelou

CHABLIS

AND

ME

INTRODUCTION
BY JOHN BERENDT

IT IS NOT enough to say that Chablis is a drag queen, or even that she is a *black* drag queen. She is both, of course, but she is much more. She is a gifted comedienne whose humor is instinctive and whose power to amuse comes from exquisite timing, a flair for the outrageous, and—I trust she'll forgive me for saying so—balls.

Chablis is a full-time transvestite. In clinical terms, she is a preoperative transsexual. She takes hormones to enlarge her breasts, but she has not had surgery and does not plan to. Like most people who take extraordinary measures to recreate themselves regardless of what others think, Chablis is confident and self-assured. She has always been this way in my presence—sassy and boldly assertive—since the first moment I laid eyes on her ten years ago that day in Savannah as I was parking my car. Her first words to me were, "Ooooo, *child!* You are right on time, honey." Now that I think of it, they could just as easily have been my first words to *her*, because within moments she had climbed into my car, into my life, and—happily for both of us—into the book I was just then writing about Savannah, *Midnight in the Garden of Good and Evil*. She simply commandeered me and my car and insisted I take her home. And then as I drove her home, she introduced herself in the most dramatic fashion possible.

"I'm Chablis," she said.

"Chablis? That's pretty," I said. "What's your full name."

"*The Lady* Chablis," she said. "It's a stage name. I'm a show-girl. I dance, I do lip synch, and I emcee. Shit like that. Mama got the name Chablis off a wine bottle. She didn't think it up for me though. It was supposed to be for my sister. Mama got pregnant when I was sixteen, and she wanted a little girl. She was gonna name her La Quinta Chablis. But then she had a miscarriage, and

I said, 'Oooh *Chablis*. That's nice. I like that name.' And Mama said, 'Then take it, baby. Call yourself Chablis from now on.' So ever since then, I've been Chablis."

"And what was your name before that?" I asked.

"Frank," she said.

As Chablis would be the first to tell you, not all drag queens are alike. There are "camp" drag queens, who put on dresses for a joke and don't bother to shave their legs or mustaches. There are "glamour" drag queens, who earnestly strive to look like women, but some do it only occasionally, while others, like Chablis, don't own a single item of men's clothing. Even among the serious, full-time drag queens, there are differences in approach. "The girls in Atlanta are full of silicone and foam-rubber hips stuck into their panty hose," says Chablis with a touch of contempt. "My titties are real. That's what my estrogen shots do for me."

Chablis knows who she is. She has taken enough trouble to create herself, so there is no ambiguity, no stumbling over pronouns. Chablis is not a he. She is not an it. She is a *she*. As a performer, she does more than wear glittering gowns, dance, and do lip synch; she takes a microphone and talks. Her monologues are spontaneous and hilarious. She banters with the audience, and when she speaks about herself, she does so with a disarming irony that has become her trademark. "I am not what I may appear to be," she will say with apparent candor, adding, "No, child, I am a heterosexual white woman. That's right, honey. Do not be fooled by what you see. When you look at me, you are lookin' at the Junior League. You are lookin' at an uptown white woman, and a pregnant uptown white woman, at that."

Chablis is a performance artist who is her own work of art. She is well aware that she has created an illusion, and she takes great pains to maintain it. "I am always careful to behave in a feminine manner," she says, "on stage and off. For instance, before I cuss someone out, I always look in the mirror to make sure I'm beautiful. Then I start cussin'." She has become an expert on changing fashions. "Wigs are fine," she says. "Anyone can wear a wig today. All the big stars wear them. Curly ones, straight ones, frizzy ones, wigs down to your shoulders, wigs down to your ass. But if you wear a wig, girl, just make sure you have that bitch pinned down. It is not a pretty sight when your wig falls off in public. And it sure as hell is not a pretty sight when it is *snatched* off, either. My advice is you should never wear a wig unless you can fight in it." In affairs of the heart, Chablis always stands by her man: "If any of you bitches lays a hand on my husband, I will smother you with my gaff*."

Upon publication of *Midnight*, in January 1994, Chablis became a media darling. She was shown on *Good Morning America*, strutting her stuff and joking with the audience at Club One in Savannah, where she performs. She went on *Oprah*, where she explained with infinite grace that her brand of female impersonation was a tribute to women, not a parody. *The New York Times* remarked that for her cameo appearance on stage at a Lincoln Center jazz concert, she made "the evening's grandest entrance." Chablis told *USA Today* that she intended to play herself in the movie version of *Midnight*, warning, "If they don't hire me, there will be no movie!"

Chablis has become a major tourist attraction in Savannah. Busloads of visitors, most of whom have never set foot in a gay club before, crowd into Club One to see her. She has even been obliged to schedule an early show so senior citizens can catch her act before bedtime. "This is my PG show," she tells them. "I'm cuttin' down on the raunchy stuff just for you!"—and she does, but only slightly.

In Savannah, Chablis's celebrity has approached the level of superstardom. The city has taken her to its heart. School children, couples and society ladies all troop in to see her. She is asked for her autograph wherever she goes. However, when she applied for permission to ride on a special float in last year's St. Patrick's Day parade, along with other characters from *Midnight*, the parade committee said no. She thereupon announced that she

---

*gaff: An item of intimate wearing apparel. For further details, see *Midnight in the Garden of Good and Evil*, J. Berendt (New York: Random House, 1994) pp. 117–118.

would "crash the damn parade." Parade officials, recalling Chablis's surprise appearance at the black debutante ball, as reported in *Midnight*, were unnerved, which was just what she wanted. She let them suffer in anticipation, but she was only toying with them.

Chablis well understood how fame would change her life. "First of all, it's going to make my price go up," she told the *Savannah Morning News*. And it did. Way up. Before *Midnight*, she made $250 a week, plus tips. Now she has a business manager, a lawyer, an agent, and a bodyguard—not to mention a checking account, a credit card, a retirement plan, and a mobile phone. In order to protect her now-famous stage name from expropriation by another drag queen, she went into court and legally changed her name to The Lady Chablis, thereby becoming, I suspect, the first person in America whose first name is "The."

Today, despite all the attention, Chablis is essentially the same Chablis she was when I met her standing on the curb ten years ago. Just as sassy, just as conniving, just as outrageous.

The mobile phone has made a difference, though. Chablis spends a great deal of time on the road, traveling from gig to gig. Now she is always in touch. "I keep my mobile phone within reach at all times," she says. "Wherever I am, my mobile phone is never further away from me than my pussy."

One afternoon not long ago I dialed Chablis's mobile-phone number, and she answered after the second ring.

"Where are you this time?" I asked.

"None of your damn business," she said, with more sass than anger. Then she lowered her voice to a conspiratorial pitch: "To tell you the truth, me and the girls are havin' us a little sewing bee."

Chablis had told me about these sewing parties. When one of the drag queens in her circle was competing in a beauty pageant, she and the other drag queens would gather at one of their houses, with fried chicken and hunch-punch, to form an assembly line for the purpose of making a fancy-dress ball gown, particularly if the gown was to be covered with thousands of bugle beads. One person would thread hundreds of needles; another would knot the thread and coat it with beeswax to make it stronger, a third would string the bugle beads on the thread, and two or three others would sew the beads to the dress.

"Are you waxing the thread today or stringing the beads?" I asked.

"Uh-uh, honey. It's not a bugle-bead party this time. We're not doing a dress today. We are making alterations on a whole damn wardrobe!" She laughed mischievously.

"For the last few months, I've had a new boyfriend," she said. "I don't know if I told you about him. Ron. A blond hunk. Well, three weeks ago Ron up and left me! Yes, child, the hunk has done dropped The Doll and is now goin' out with a real woman— a *biological* female. But The Doll is not about to take this lying down. Sistuh is striking back! Which is why, at this very moment, me and the girls are here in the new girlfriend's house while the bitch is off at work. I am serious. We jimmied the back door open and brought in five sewing machines! And we are takin' in all the bitch's clothes—tightening everything half an inch. Every damn skirt, blouse, dress, pants, and jeans she owns. See, I happen to know Ron likes his women on the slim side. Girlfriend has a tendency to put on weight. She's gonna freak out when she comes home and tries to cram herself into any of this shit, 'cause it's all gonna be reeeeal tight, even her panties and bras. 'Cause us five little ol' seamstresses be sewin' our damn asses off. It's like a sweatshop in here. I am serious." I could hear the sewing machines whirring in the background.

"Do you think she'll be fooled by it?"

"Just you watch," said Chablis. "Bright and early tomorrow morning, girlfriend's gonna be rushing to the supermarket, loading up on Optifast and Slim-Fast and Dexitrim and Jenny Craig and buyin' videotapes of Miss Richard Simmons's exercise classes. She's gonna be running up and down that StairMaster, and starving herself, and gettin' all mean and short-tempered. Then, just when she slims down enough so she fits into her clothes, me and my sewing circle is gonna break in here again and tighten everything another half inch. Y-e-e-e-s, *child!* Girlfriend's gonna be one angry bag of bones when we get finished with her."

"And then Ron will come running back to The Doll," I said.

"You get the picture, honey."

"And once again The Doll will get what she wants."

"Gettin' what she wants is what The Doll is all about," said Chablis. "It's what *women* are all about, in case you didn't know. And, after all, The Doll…is…a…woman!"

—JOHN BERENDT
NEW YORK CITY
JANUARY, 1996

HIDING MY CANDY

THE NEGRO

SCARLETT

O'HARA

PROLOGUE

Y'WOULDN'T KNOW who I am unless you've read that book *Midnight in the Garden of Good and Evil* by John Berendt. Or seen me on *Good Morning America*. Or the *Today Show*. Or *Oprah*. Or read about me and seen my picture in *People* magazine. Or *USA Today*. Or *Entertainment Weekly*. And while I'm on the subject, if you haven't caught my act in any of those places, child, where in the *hell* have you been?

But that's okay. Do not let it bother you if you are a total ignoramus on the subject of me—otherwise known as The Doll, y'mama, The Lady Chablis—because I'm fixin' to change all that. I do recommend you read *Midnight*, 'cause it's one hell of a good book—*but not now!* Now it's time to pay full attention to y'mama. *Midnight*—or The Book, as they call it in Savannah—can wait till later. All you have to know about it for now is that I am the outrageously charming black drag queen who stole the two best chapters in it: "The Grand Empress of Savannah" and "Black Minuet." John Berendt wrote about me as one of the many quirky folks who helped make Savannah such a kinky background for the bigger story he was telling: the shocking murder case of *Miss* Jim Williams and his humpy white Georgia-cracker boyfriend, Danny Hansford. John probably thought of me as a minor character, but as The Doll proved to him and his readers, she is not—I repeat: N O T—a minor anything.

When we last encountered each other in John's book, it was early June of 1987, and he was asking—no, make that *imploring*—y'mama to leave the Alpha Debutante Cotillion, which he felt she'd somehow *crashed*. I guess John was worried that his reputation with the black society snobs of Savannah, who host this annual bash, might get tarnished some if they knew him and me was friends. That's understandable. Most folks—black or white—have a hard time realizing that underneath all the shimmer and sass, I'm really just y'typical Ivory girl. I think John was mostly concerned that I might do something *compromising*. Well...I sure proved him right, didn't I?

But hell, bitch, that wasn't the point. My first upper-crust black-folk gig wasn't gonna be undone by some *damn* Yankee writer from New York. No, no. The Doll may be a heterosexual white woman in mind, but her black body and soul belong to Miss Rosa Parks, girl. Yes, ma'am. She lives by one rule alone: what Miss Thang wants, Miss Thang gets!

Now, I ain't kiddin' when I recount that all eyes was fixed on y'mama when she entered that ballroom. These folks did not expect the likes of *my* arrival, and I don't think they'd seen this much sparkling since the Supremes first went on *The Ed Sullivan Show*. So, was I a li'l *obvious* in my blue, rhinestoned gown with a slit that was *showin' off* y'mama's legs? Well, I knew I was fixing to give more than a few of 'em a jolt of my immodesty. But they were *not* what you'd call a Motown crowd neither, so I also had to adjust my attitude some, according to protocol, and tone down the sizzle. At least till I'd had myself a drink.

I also regarded this night as *my* debut in black society, so I played up the persona of Lady Mystique to the hilt, sashaying about with a regal stride as I looked round at a room fulla strangers I'd prob'ly never see again. I could tell by the grinning stares that I mighta been the feast of desire for some of those men. But I was the one who was hungry. And thirsty. When The Doll finally spotted Mr. John Berendt, he was sitting at his assigned table chatting with a bunch of the light-skinned kind so popular among the parishioners of St. Matthew's Episcopal Church. That's right, baby—that black place of *status* worship here in Savannah, where people act like uptown wannabe white folks.

So I confidently made my way over to John.

"Don't y'say or do nothing 'bout me bein' here, 'cause if y'do, I'll tell 'em all!" I said to him in a discreet but defiant whisper. I wasn't standing there long before my eyes suddenly averted to a lone gentleman directly behind us. "Excuse me, y'all," I interrupted, "*but I recognize an ol' friend lookin' for me.*"

Oooh, child! The muscular object of my distraction stood looking as bored as a whore in a convent. Well, girl, that made two of us, though the evening was about to take a swift turn for the better.

"Pardon me, but the line at the bar is a *mile* long, and a li'l bitty thing like me's apt to get trampled," I said, vamping it up with my hand on my hip and extending an empty glass I'd picked up as a prop. "Would y'mind...?" His brows arched as he lurched to fulfill my request before I had a chance to finish my bullshit. I smiled graciously and fluttered my lids, convinced that mascara and eyeliner were a girl's only dependable friends under dim lighting.

Naturally, he obliged with the kinda eagerness most men display when they meet me. So when he bowed to kiss my hand and placed his left arm behind his back like a butler, I thought he was *wearin' it out*! Very smooth, he was. And suave, too, the way he towered elegantly in his tuxedo. He was like Shaft meets 007. Oooh, somebody needed to shake The Doll quick, 'cause she was some kinda stirred!

"I'm Philip, by the way," he said, tilting forward on his toes as he warned, "Don't go away on me, now." As if *that* was likely. No, baby. I stood froze with *an-ti-ci-pa-tion*, while his deep butch voice and his big ol' fine self made a beeline for one of them crowded bars. *Lord, can that boy serve it*, I mused as I watched those broad shoulders turning, drinks in hand, en route back to the belle of the ball.

Oooh, he was a gorgeous thing, y'might recall. A lighter shade of cocoa, and the prettiest gray eyes y'mama'd ever saw. I was salivating, child. His thick hair was a mix of black and reddish tint, which I'd hoped wasn't some sort of henna—y'know, like maybe a suggestion that Mr. Man was a big ol' sissy. Can't always tell these days, honey! At six-feet tall, the boy was some kinda strapping. Come to learn, too, that he was just nineteen years old, but that was okay, 'cause The Doll's rocked more than a couple cradles in her time.

He kindly introduced me to his sister LaVella, who was one of the debutantes. She seemed smart and career-oriented, y'might say, which compensated for her lack of *glamour*. Oooh, *somebody* needed to teach this girl how to be fem'nine. How to pluck her eyebrows and tweeze that hair off her lip. Girlfriend was eight miles of bad road, from the nun's neckline of her tacky new dress right down to those Li'l Debbie Snackin' Cake pumps. Y'know, the kind with the *itsy-bitsy* heel?

The Doll, on the other hand, looked damn good! As if that should come as any surprise. Turning heads, she was, left and *right*, child! She was having herself a fine ol' time, what with all them other black boys giving her *fe-e-e-ver*! Yeah, there were gangs of 'em—those escorts—huddled 'bout like a football team, just waiting for me to walk by and pretend to trip. I honestly can't recall the last time so many men gave y'mama such a collective good time while she was standing up. It was obvious them estrogen shots was working *time-and-a-half*. I was successfully hiding my candy! Y'know, *my T, my Truth*.

Which has always been my biggest fear, 'cause the black folks can clock y'quicker than the white folks, and children'll getcha in a minute! I don't know how it is that them folks can spot a drag queen, but it's one of the reasons I kinda stay away from the black community. And it's also why I don't babysit. Li'l kids have an amazing sixth sense. Just ask any other drag queen, honey, and she'll tell y'the same thing.

Why, just earlier that same day, I was standing in the ten-items-or-less line at the Piggly Wiggly, and I was trying to be all *fishy-poo*: Miss Brenda Dale Knox, as I'm legally known outta face. There I was, absorbed in my *National Enquirer,* when I peered out briefly to check the progress of the line, only to notice the li'l blond boy at his mama's skirt standing in front of me and looking up with his mouth wide open.

"Hey, cutie," I cooed maternally. "Why y'so *shy*? Come here, child, and gimme a kiss." I crouched down to his pint size and doted on him like I was his auntie Chablis.

"I ain't givin' y'no kiss, boy," he fired, fast as a pistol, and released my hand from his shoulder with a sharp shrug. The kid continued to glare at me.

Well, crack my face, baby! There I was thinking I was *The Doll,* all fabulousness and fem'ninity. But the jig was up, girl. *It was official!* And he couldn't have been no more than six years old. Nope. Nobody else in that grocery store knew who or what I was, but *that* li'l boy sure did.

But now, back at the debutante ball, my senses were reminded that tonight, anyway, I'd managed to conceal any evidence that I might be something other than the ravishing creature I presented to all these fancy folks. I wasn't necessarily looking to land a wealthy husband, and none of this was ever intended as a matter of deception. But considering some of the scares The Doll's had over the years, she can never be too rich, too thin, or too careful.

When Philip took me home from the ball, we sat snugly for an hour in the velveteen comfort of his new Mercury Cougar and talked all about me. Then, I s'ppose, we talked a li'l 'bout him. Told me that he'd sorta had a girlfriend but it wasn't serious, and I told him about Jeff, the blond hunk I was seeing at the time I made it into the pages of John Berendt's book. Then, just as my right silver slipper made its way outta the car door, I slipped Philip my phone number. Y'can be sure he called the next day.

At thirty years of age, and for only the second time in my adult life, I was faced with dating a man who had absolutely no clue 'bout me. Most of the men I'd ever been involved with had some notion of my show life, but Philip was young and some kinda wholesome. He had the nice-family thing going on. And I was so afraid I might lose this wonderful friend that I remained a lady and never let on 'bout anything that might give myself away. But then when things began to get serious between us, he started pressing for more than just a good-night kiss.

"Now, that's why I don't date black boys, 'cause that's all they want," I'd tell him. Then he'd apologize profusely, saying that *I* was in the driver's seat and that I should let him know what the signs read along our highway of love. Well, I guess he didn't want The Doll to arrest him for speeding.

So, nervous as I was of ever hurting him, I kept using those excuses till I got *so* hot and *so* bothered and *so* ready to give it up that I knew, girl, it had to be T-time. Now, I thought long and hard 'bout this: I couldn't tell him on the phone, 'cause it wouldn't be fair. Couldn't tell him to his face, 'cause he might lose it and harm me. Write him a letter? No, somebody else might get ahold of it. I had to handle this matter carefully, so I came up with a plan: I'd ask him out for a night on the town, completely at my expense.

Understand, The Doll meant business here, 'cause the only time she grabs for her purse in the company of a man is to touch up her lipstick. But I didn't wanna blow this, so I made a reservation at Garibaldi's—my favorite restaurant in Savannah and, I might add, one of the city's finest—and took a very deep breath. Then, just for good measure, I hightailed my ass over to church to light a candle.

Needless to say, I looked *flawless* when he arrived to get me. That was one department I had covered, thanks to Miss Dawn DuPree, my drag sister and seamstress, who'd just made me a champagne-colored satin cocktail number that came down just above my knee. Sweetheart neck, shoulders exposed. And a satin stole to match. It was lovely, child, but it was also the dead of winter, and even in the warmer climate of the South, I had no business wearing that dress in public. But I figured if the visuals didn't knock him out, the fumes from Yves Saint-Laurent's Rive Gauche were sure to, seeing as I was wearing half the bottle.

Now, despite my delicate frame, I can eat just like Nell Carter when I want, and on this night of nights my appetite was huge! 'Course y'know how white folks' restaurants are, honey—they only give y'one tablespoon of food—so even though I was some kinda starved, I had to play it dainty and poke at my Caesar salad like a good uptown white woman would. Philip liked watching me eat, though mostly, I think he was delighted with himself for scoring an older woman. I musta also given him this *worldly* illusion of me, even though the truth was I'd never been west of the Mississippi.

"I'm old enough to put y'over my knee," I'd tease whenever he'd ask my age. He seemed intrigued by the prospect of a spanking, but like the gentleman he was, he never allowed y'mama's flirtation to be mistaken for a green light to her pussy; which was now calling her for the other reason—*nature*.

Miss Bathroom wasn't too kind to that procedure on this particular evening, 'cause a girl like me will *not* use public rest rooms if there's multiple stalls inside. The Doll needs privacy. She can't be pulling and tugging in the face of fish. Know what I'm saying, child? Y'mama don't want to have to *readjust* her candy and her ovaries trying to get her gaff back up, which takes time and a decent mirror to make sure things are where they need to be! She will use the public bathroom for powdering *only*, if it ain't a single-stall operation.

If I really gotta pee bad and can't wait for the fish to swim, I *do* make sure that when I squat, I imitate the way women turn their feet to the side or curl their toes forward just as they roll the t.p. to wipe. It's just a thing I've noticed that women do in the stalls. It must enable 'em to spread their legs a li'l more to keep the pee from leaking—the same way guys *shake it* once they're done.

Well, I managed to steal a few seconds of quiet time in the ladies' room and then hurried back out to Philip. We continued to sip the last of our bottle of Asti Spumante as we nursed our third round of now-diluted whiskey sours that we'd ordered before our entrées. Laughing and sharing glances with me, he seemed giddy enough for me to pop the question: Had he ever heard of the Pickup?

"Isn't that a *gay* bar?" he returned with a look of anxiety. (Savannah's a small enough town that y'don't have to frequent a place to know its reputation.) In the seconds that passed between our exchange, I reminded myself again that it was now or never. I plied him with a fresh drink and a li'l more girlish enticing. Then I asked our waiter for the check.

When we got to the Pickup, Philip was so self-conscious: he kept fiddling with his tie and held on to me like a parachute, just in case anybody there thought he was after the same thing they were. 'Course, I'd already warned the folks that I worked with that when we walked in, I wasn't gonna stop to say hello. I had to pretend like it was my first time there, too, if I was gonna pull this off with Philip's feelings intact. As much as I hated myself for it, I had to ignore some of my fans, too, even though the waiters had been ordered to tell 'em all that I wasn't to be disturbed with autographs and pictures till *after* my show.

We flew on past the congestion of sissy-biker types, dressed in head-to-toe black leather, that were crowding the bar area, and just as we spotted a quiet table in the corner, I heard the familiar strains of the overture from *Man of La Mancha* starting up. I told Philip to go sit down while I hit the ladies' room and that I'd be right back. Instead, y'mama rushed back to the dressing room faster than OJ once moved through airports. After all, she still had to put on some heavier makeup, her false eyelashes, a long-haired wig, and the nastiest, shortest, *skankiest* dress she owned. If Philip thought I looked *fine* at the black debutante cotillion, wait till he saw me on stage in a room full of white folks!

"Tonight y'gotta announce me as the South's *number-one* female impersonator, The *Lady* Chablis," I ordered 'em backstage. I was usually hailed, "The Toast of the South," but I wanted a more descriptive intro for my baby's sake. Figured it would soften the blow some if he saw what a big star he was dating. And that's what they gave me.

When I shimmied out from behind the curtain, I was a blaze of glitter. I launched into Gladys Knight's "Midnight Train to Georgia" to the deafening applause of my fans, who were whistling, howling, yelling, and hooting, while the sequins on my dress was nailing 'em with retina damage. Well, child, not four bars into the song, these folks began queuing up like they was the Pips themselves. When each of 'em approached the stage, I'd lean down just enough to give their wallets proximity to my body. A kiss for each single issue of currency, and a whiff of my pussy scent for a twenty-dollar bill. Now, that sounds like a Wal-Mart bargain to me!

But in the midst of all this attention I was getting from my fans, I saw my stallion stand up from the corner table and storm outta the club.

"...*bought a one-way ticket back to the life he once knew...*"

Philip fled faster than a fugitive. Imagine my surprise after all of that trouble I'd gone to just to spare his emotions. But I wasn't gonna allow this distraction to throw off my rhythm. *Leave it to y'mama to put her trials and tribulations into her act!* I wanted my fans to help me. They were my support system. My gift to them is laughter. That's right baby: laugh y'ass off, forget y'problems—that's why *I* am here. Thankfully enough, the crowd's satisfaction with my performance gave me something other than Philip's abrupt exit to think about. Besides, he wasn't paying my bills; they were. And hell, bitch, I still had a second show to do!

"*Good evenin'*, ladies and gentlemen—and the rest of you *bitches!*"

"HEY BITCH!" they shouted back.

"Thank y'all for bein' here tonight." All kinds of whistling was piercing my applause. "To those of you who arrived promptly, I say, 'Thank you very much,' and to those of you who didn't: 'You bitches can kiss my ass!'"

"Lemme kiss it!" a frat boy yelled out from the back-left corner, interrupting The Doll's monologue.

"Tuna eggs might be cheap, but this brand of caviar'll cost ya, bitch!" Oooh, that shut Mr. Sigma *fuckin'* Chi right up. "Yeah, y'wanna kiss it and smell it, just like that boy who done just walked outta here thought he was gonna do. Didja catch that flagrant display of *disrespect* for y'mama?"

"What happened?" bellowed several audience members.

"Gimme a damn minute and I'll tell ya what happened. That man took her Ladyship on a date earlier this evenin', *wined and dined her he did,* and thought that alone would entitle him to father her child! But he musta saw all them men's mouths waterin' and realized he had to take a number! *And get this one*—the cheap asshole didn't even *tip* The Doll!"

"Lynch the sonofabitch!" shouted that drunken refugee from *Animal House.*

"Why don't I lynch you instead?" Silence. "Y'all better remember that the sign on my pussy says 'Members *Only.'* I ain't *givin' it away,* bitches!"

The next day when I woke up with a hangover—my eyes cringing from more than just the stream of sunlight parading through my bedroom curtains—reality struck. I thought, God, that man must be devastated. He must be some kinda hurt—*or ready to kick my ass!* Should I find him? Should I call him? Should I put a note on his car? Ah, I decided to just leave it alone and let him sweat it.

When I finally heard from him about two weeks later, I was more than a bit relieved, but I was also scared shitless. I kept wondering what surprises *he* was gonna pull.

"This friend of mine gave me some pot and..." Philip's voice trailed off nervously on the telephone. "...I know you like to smoke...."

I said nothing as I held the phone and surveyed the chipped

purple nail color I'd sampled at Rich's only days before.

"So why don't I come by and we'll go for a ride?"

"Are y'*sure*?" The Doll asked, understandably suspicious.

"Yeah, I'm sure," he said softly, like he was ready to pout or something. I knew deep in my heart that he believed I was really a woman. So regardless of my T, he wasn't gonna punish me without being mindful of my fem'nine condition.

He beeped the horn twice, and I got in gingerly with just enough reflex coordination to retrace my steps in case he got mean. We sat in his car for a while, not moving from the street outside my apartment house. Neither of us was saying very much, 'cept for superficial stuff that would prevent us both from having to take the plunge first. He motioned for me to open the glove compartment, and I took out the bag of reefer and proceeded to roll a very fat cigarette. I studied the design of the E-Z Wider package so that I wouldn't have to look up at him. Should I just apologize and get it over with? Hmmm. That was impossible. The Doll ain't never sorry for being she.

Maybe it was the reefer, but my paranoia got the better of me, and I was afraid I wouldn't know how to defend myself without looking like a villainess. As Philip quietly exhaled, I looked out my window, refusing the last of the joint he handed my way. I could feel his eyes in my direction several times, but I still kept quiet. So did he. That is, till we pulled round the playground that sits in the middle of Crawford Square, where I lived.

"You made a fool outta me!" he began to lash out once we hit Abercorn Street, downtown Savannah's main artery to the suburbs and beyond. The Doll held her silent ground till finally her native testosterone got fed up and told her estrogen shots to take a hike!

"So what's the *problem*?" I demanded, turning the tables and looking him straight in the eye. No reaction. "I never *used* you or *conned* you, if that's what y'think!" I really did care what this fella thought of me.

"But you're a man...." he said in a cracked voice, straining to convince himself.

"Well, as far as I'm concerned, Philip, I'm all *woman*." And with that y'mama tore open her blouse and revealed her titties as evidence. He grazed 'em with a steady pause as The Doll continued proving her case. "I will *not* be labeled, Philip."

"But why did you lie to me?"

"It's not as cut-and-dried as that," I reasoned. "I didn't wanna gamble away one of the best friends I've made in years. And besides, I'd have missed out on all o' that *winin' and dinin'*." Well, with that winning line, I got him to smile. Yes, child, The Doll is self-centered—that's just part of her charm. I s'ppose that once Philip got over the fact that I was *not* clockable and that no one was calling *him* into question just for being my friend, the verdict was in, child, and The Doll got herself an acquittal.

After this conversation, Philip and me decided that we were always gonna remain friends, regardless of whether folks round him learned the truth about me. Or whether he ever gave me any of that candy. I made sure that he was gonna come away from this experience respecting me. So what if he couldn't show me his affection voluntarily no more? It was still visible in his heart.

And as far as sex goes? Well, that *woulda* changed everything between us. But, girl, lemme tell you—we came real close on one occasion, 'cause his lingering curiosity was just as piqued as his initial anger. But y'mama was strong, child. I knew if we'd done something, we wouldn't've felt as comfortable round each other ever again; and my presence would always be reminding him of that. Just as he'd always be reminding me of what I was. *Of what I am.*

DADDY'S

LI'L GIRL

CHAPTER 1

I WAS BORN Benjamin Edward Knox at Gadsden County Memorial Hospital in Quincy, Florida, on March 11, 1957, at 2:10 AM. On one whole block of downtown, in the middle of a park that's loaded with azalea bushes, sits a big, beautiful ol' courthouse made of stucco that stands four stories high. Behind this central building is Highway 90, the old road that still connects us to Tallahassee, our closest "big city" by twenty miles. When I was born, us *colored* folks lived on the other side of that highway, which now runs parallel with the new interstate and that same ol' courthouse along Jefferson Street.

My home was with Gran'mama, Miss Anna Mae Ponder, who always smelled like the fresh lavender that was her one indulgence and sported a smile no matter what. A feeling of tranquillity, love, and strength would prevail as fast as I caught sight of her. Never one to argue with anybody, Gran'mama didn't believe in raising her hand or her voice. The quiet dignity that still prevails in Gran'mama's world set the tone for the way we lived.

I guess many gran'mamas are prob'ly like mine: they don't ever age in y'mind, 'cause they have a dependable way of looking like y'fondest memory of 'em. Gran'mama's perfectly rolled steel-gray hair still shimmers from beneath a black net, and her silver cat's-eye glasses with their jeweled fins have never been replaced *or* updated. She's also blessed with something that most black folks have way over white folks: the fact that they age a helluva lot more gracefully. Child, I've got blouses with more wrinkles than she'll ever have.

My real mama was only there for a few months after she birthed me. That's a few months longer than my daddy stayed. Mama'd done moved to Chicago to go to nursing school, I was often told, and her ambitions were understandably accountable for her absence in my early life. She telephoned Gran'mama regularly, but she never returned in the flesh till I was nine. That's three years before my daddy's first appearance, too. From my infancy till about the age of six, my companion, my protector, and my *mama* was her sister, my aunt Katie Bell, a plainly pretty woman of average weight for a somebody who's five-foot-five and whose goodness was as natural as the mole on her chin. A real mama in every sense of the word, she diapered me and fed me and even nursed me on her dry titties. Since she lived close by, she took me everywhere with her. So, whether she was playing cards at

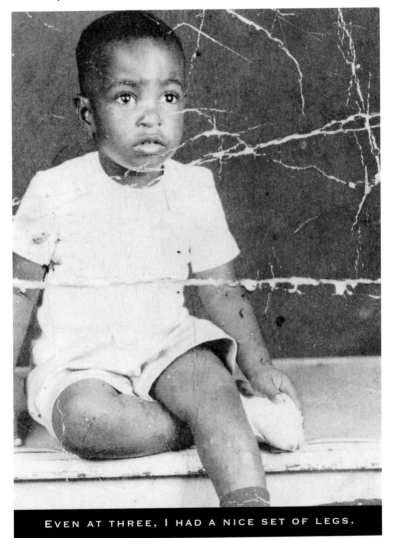

EVEN AT THREE, I HAD A NICE SET OF LEGS.

Walton's Juke Joint, buying nylons at the Woolworth, or off dancing with my uncle Lonnie, there I'd be right alongside her hip.

While I didn't really grow up in poverty, I do remember that Gran'mama struggled some while raising her three other daughters and me; though let it be said that my family never wanted for nothing. And never took a handout from nobody, 'cept for the occasional kindness of Gran'mama's employers, the Ashleys, a middle-aged doctor and his wife. She worked as their maid during the early 1960s of my youth; and she always wore the same gray-and-white uniform that TV's Hazel did.

Gran'mama's greatest gift to our family wasn't just the support involved in caring for us all; it was also the example she set by her nurturing of friendship and her charity toward others. She taught us early that it doesn't cost a penny to be nice and what's returned in the bargain is often priceless. Typically Gran'mama, she found virtues in all kinds of folks, but never made mention of her own. Her modesty and grace—two qualities The Doll herself sometimes loses to amnesia—were underscored by her pride and determination. She made damn sure her daughters knew that there was a future for them, and that's why my aunts all went to the local college. And that's also why they was always living with Gran'mama.

Our house was a big ol' wooden rectangle, its dirty-white exterior chipping and peeling on all four sides. It was here that Gran'mama once lived with my gran'daddy, who'd left her a widow ten years before I was born. Nothing glamorous 'bout this place I first called home—no plumbing even—but it was solid like the foundation Gran'mama set for our family. The house had itself a boxed appendage of a porch, windowless and centered on our front door. A swing and some garden chairs in a rusted array of fifties pastel green were scattered for us to sit on during the summer months. Our property sat some thirty feet from the road, surrounded by a thick mass of wild vegetation and overgrown shrubs. This was our home on Lincoln Street.

The strongest sensual images of my childhood are of that first house and the constant aromas from the kitchen and the wood-stove fireplace, mixing as effortlessly as the neighborhood folks who'd drop on by for a helping of Gran'mama's cuisine. "One li'l oxtail and a spoonful o' rice, that's all I got f'you, so enjoy it!" So spoke Gran'mama as she'd prepare a plate of food for anybody hungry. That's the spirit in which I was raised. Open y'doors. Open y'hearts. *Open y'fridge.*

Quincy is characteristic of lotsa Southern towns in attitude, but it doesn't have that Floridian look of palm trees and all of that. This was inland Florida, and while we've got plenty of oak and magnolia trees to shade us, there's no major body of water, just li'l lakes here and there, so it gets very hot and very dry in the summer. Now, I can't say this climate helped The Doll's sultry complexion none, but then again, she hadn't yet discovered her moisturizers. And in the meantime, girl, her preoccupations were oriented toward other things. Like the local Baptist church.

Sunday services were a major part of our lives. It was an all-day affair, and that was just fine with me. It was my time to perform, see: I was an usher and, impressively, an *Assistant Superintendent of the sunday school.* I was the kid selected to make all the speeches and social announcements in front of the crowd. The congregation loved that as much as I did, 'cause they knew I was gonna give 'em *gestures* with it. My emphasis was on *performance,* honey—standing tall and stabbing away at elocution—regardless of whether the message was 'bout Bingo Night or the monthly church picnic. So, was this where The Doll first learned to perfect her stage presence? Well, it was certainly where she learned to monopolize an audience!

I was the first *openly and flamboyantly* "gay" person I knew of in my hometown. That being the way, I guess I was protected by my family, much the way a retarded child is looked after. I mean, Gran'mama knew I was a *sissy,* and while I don't think she liked it, her boundless love for me would never have allowed her to harp on the fact that I needed to make drastic changes. Besides, she didn't believe in tampering with what was purely the Lord's business. And she made sure I knew that a higher power ultimately called the shots.

From very early on I guess, it was my strong, abiding faith in Jesus Christ above that helped me understand myself most, at least according to the ways that I felt I was "different" from the other li'l boys. As far as I could reckon, and no matter what any-

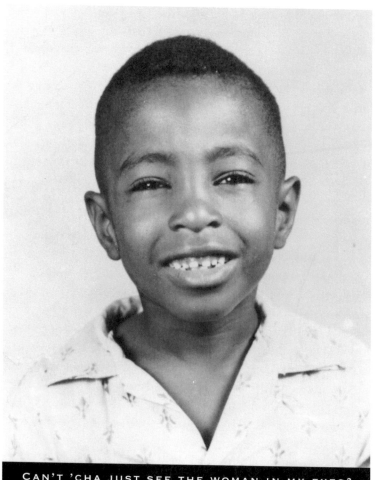

body else thought, I was really a li'l girl—*with candy*—just like the Lord had instructed. At times, of course, this would all seem a li'l confusing when society was expecting me to behave in a way that conflicted with my heart. But even back then, I didn't pay society any more mind than I do now.

'Round my sixth birthday we moved *uptown*—actually eight blocks away—to our new house, which wasn't any bigger, just more *modern*, 'cause it had an indoor toilet and it sat on a concrete foundation. We had a screened-in porch that y'walked up three steps to, and these led to the front door. The first thing that caught my eye was the curved design of those stairs—and how good I'd look *posing* on them. I think you'd call this place a "raised ranch." I called it clean and *white*. Gleaming white. And it made me think we was going places, though we almost never left the territory that marked our black neighborhood. In fact, my childhood world was so tiny that not till junior high did I ever have a reason to cross Highway 90. Our new house was destiny enough for The Doll.

At home, Gran'mama preferred her entertainment from a radio whose tuner was perm'nently glued to the gospel station. Her evening domain was an overstuffed chair in a marigold plaid that belonged to her alone. She sat there quietly with her companion cup of coffee and other faithful forms of recreation: the daily newspaper and her Bible. My bedtime was nine o'clock on most nights, maybe later on a weekend, but only if we had a house full of folks over to play pinochle. Besides, I usually needed my beauty rest if I was gonna rise with the sun and be out the door exploring the wild grasses round Gran'mama's house.

Nature was my best friend, see, and my sense of amusement and curiosity—well before I ever knew what *candy* was—mostly came from the li'l creek behind our house that transported me to other worlds within my 'magination. I relished the ritual that became my daily communication with what I *perceived* was the rest of the planet. Every day I'd take all the nearby leaves that several ancient oaks had showered from their branches and write my name on them or maybe my initials and our address, then, one by one, I'd stagger this scribbled parade as I sent 'em off downstream.

"I wonder if they made it," I'd always sweetly wonder. Then I'd sit back and dream they were en route to Paris or Africa or whatever country we was studying that week at Stevens Elementary School. I just knew they had to have gone farther than 717 Seventh Street, but where exactly was anybody's guess. I even waited in vain for the courtesy of a reply, though I s'ppose I got some satisfaction thinking that folks all over the world knew just where to find me in Quincy.

Sometimes I'd take to varying my li'l routine with an empty matchbox that I'd inscribe with an anonymous "I love you." While nowadays The Doll can still be found practicing this li'l gesture with gorgeous strangers in nightclubs coast-to-coast, back then she was pressing to find something more than just an amusement. But as much as I loved Gran'mama, I also needed a male role model in my life, and I became more conscious of this when we moved to that new house. *Where are the men?* I musta thought, knowing that something was always different about the Ponder household, which was only filled with women.

In the company of a man, I'd be jumping up and down, swishing about, and flirting up a storm. Well, girl, I can tell y'nothing's changed, but maybe back then I was just hoping any one of those men might stay for good. There was something different 'bout the way a man smelled and the way he canvassed a room with the strength of his body, waving *Good evenin', y'all* and muscling his way onto our corduroy sofa while any one of my three maiden aunts might be taking her sweet-ass time getting fixed up to party.

"Ever since y'was three years old, you be wantin' to sit up in men's laps!" Aunt Katie Bell still kids me. I useta think it mighta been just an early *sexual* attraction, but I only vaguely felt my sexual yearnings at that time. Though I do remember asking this one li'l neighborhood boy, who was prob'ly my same age of seven, to come out back with me one day so I could show him the li'l creek that was my stream of dreams. I told him the best way to look downriver was to lay on his stomach and rock back 'n' forth. Only in order to get a *real* view of the way the stream did its twist and turn, he needed to prop himself on something else to get a steadier motion. Yes, child, y'mama provided that rhythm!

"Edward? Y'come in here and help me get this bird plucked!" cried Gran'mama, who always called me by my middle name. She musta been peering through the kitchen window right then to check on us, just in case we'd drowned or something. But I knew it was really 'cause she meant to put a stop to the only sex I was ever gonna get as a child.

"Y'know, Edward, you'll have a family of y'own someday," she'd often impart, just before it led to a gentle request that I find something boyish to occupy my time with—that, say, chopping the head off a chicken was fine enough, but cooking it was something else entirely; that it was okay to help her moisturize her dry scalp, just so long as I didn't get fixed on *styling* her hair, too. These were the sweet and subtle reminders that it was all right to be helpful, just not too *do*mestic, that I'd one day have to assume the responsibilities of manhood. And, well, boyhood, in Gran'mama's eyes, seemed a fine enough place to start.

I **CAN'T TELL** y'very much about my daddy at all, 'cept that he was handsome and tall and that his name was Benjamin Franklin Knox. It occurs to me that I might be descended from one of them slaves of the real Benjamin Franklin, 'cause we all know The Doll's sure got a way with *electricity*. They called my daddy Frank, which is the name I used as my own in John Berendt's book. I fibbed a li'l, but now I'm coming clean.

My daddy came into my life on a visit once to Quincy when I was almost twelve. The first time I saw him was brief *and awkward:* I didn't know who he was outside of the fact that we were related, so I musta resented having to call him *Daddy.* Instead, I called him *sir.* The first thing I noticed 'bout him was his thick salt-'n'-pepper mustache and the smell of Old Spice all over his clothing. I never had any affection for him. Didn't want no hugs or kisses, no kinda promises of love or starting over. Too li'l, too late as far as his daughter with candy was concerned. He'd been missing for too damn long.

After that initial visit, the next thing I knew I was being sent to live with him in New York for the summer. F'sure he didn't like my girlie ways none—not that we ever talked about it directly, but y'could tell he hated it about me.

"Whatcha mean y'don't *like* baseball?" My daddy demanded to know after I frowned at going to a Yankee game my second night there. "That ain't *normal* for a li'l boy y'age!"

"I don't know nothin' 'bout baseball, sir. Don't care to, neither," I pouted, my hips leading an about-face in a sway of disgust.

He lived in New York City at Broadway and 125th Street, which was Harlem. Yeah, I may've been a sissy-hick from Florida, but I could tell from the get-go that this area was nothing but a shithole.

That summer of 1969, it was just the two of us and his girlfriend, a Latin bombshell named Lila, in his cramped one-bedroom apartment that was filled with worn-out and mismatched furniture. The place was clean thanks to her, but it reeked of smoke from his big ol' cigars, and there were lotsa empty bourbon bottles cluttering up the counter next to the kitchen sink. Lila'd taken a couple of the empty ones, washed off the labels, and stuck flowers in 'em. Hell, bitch musta thought she was the Puerto Rican Martha Stewart.

Since the decorator hadn't finished the guest room, I had to sleep on a sofa that smelled like a brewery and farted its stuffing every time I moved. Most nights, I'd lie real still while I studied the migrating patterns of the cockroaches that darted up the walls and into the shadows from a flickering neon sign just outside the living room window. Lemuel's Liquors was the ground-floor merchant in my daddy's apartment building, the source for all that bourbon. They'd stay open till midnight, way long enough for me to lose count of them roaches that kept me distracted from the sounds that came from my daddy's bedroom.

On the entertainment front, my daddy's patience was wearing thin, so he decided—on Lila's insistence—to enroll me in a sewing course at the Harlem Institute of Fashion. A friend of hers was an instructor there, so she suggested it to my daddy as something constructive for me to do during the day—prob'ly so I wouldn't be bouncing up and down Broadway like a big sissy, getting raped and killed.

The Harlem Institute of Fashion? Just like the name suggests: a big ol' room with a lotta black folks in there sewing stuff, and that was about it. My summer project turned out to be a li'l pair of trousers—*maybe they were capri pants*—and I did learn how to use a sewing machine, which would later come in handy. At least till the day I'd meet up with Miss Dawn DuPree, my seamstress.

Of all the folks I met at the Harlem Institute, I remember this one gay guy there the most. I thought he was just about the coolest thing I'd ever seen. Very fem'nine and all of that—y'know, pink ruffled shirts underneath her tight-fitting suits, lotsa *rings and bracelets*. Honey, the Age of Aquarius had surely bypassed Quincy, so up till now, jewelry for guys was only something I dreamed about. Girlfriend was my first up-close-and-personal look at what sissies grow up to be. And, child, if her wardrobe was any kinda indication, the future was looking brighter by the minute.

What I remember most about New York that summer was riding the buses and subways, listening to my daddy and Lila going at it, and eating lotsa them long, skinny hot dogs that y'couldn't get in Florida. I *think* I liked it there, but I was only a kid and, since I didn't know my daddy none, I felt uncomfortable living under his roof and ready to go home on a moment's notice. What also gnawed at me was never knowing if he'd *invited* me 'cause he wanted me in his life or whether Mama'd *forced* him to take me for a li'l while. Maybe they thought he could straighten me out. But y'know something, I still don't know why I was ever there that summer.

Today I don't have any lingering emotions 'bout my daddy, 'cause there really aren't any. The bottom line is, we never got to know each other. I resent this state of affairs some, but I choose not to dwell on what I can't change. When he died of cancer in 1984, his funeral was the next and last time I'd ever see him again. And I only went to the service 'cause I was his only child and that's what I was taught was proper.

"How dare y'show up in that getup when y'papa's lyin' dead?" yelled my daddy's sister Bessie, a woman I never knew at all. "Y'tryin' to shame us one and all?" she persisted, making a stink over a most demure li'l black dress that tastefully complemented the woman I'd become.

"That sonofabitch showed up twice in my life. Y'think he gives a shit what I'm wearin'?" I read that ol' bitch up one side and down the other. It wasn't my intention to make a scene, but I realized then that I'd no business going to the funeral of a man I barely ever saw just outta *respect*. Too many unseen years had passed, years that masked a change in my identity from somebody who that side of the family'd never really known in the first place.

I started crying and left the church. Following me from behind was my other aunt, Susie, who tried to comfort me some.

"Y'know Bessie's got a tongue on her, so never y'mind her big mouth this day. She's just grievin', baby," she offered, caressing a portion of the black silk shawl that covered my shoulders.

I stopped my weeping and looked up at her.

"I just don't get it…. *Didn't my daddy ever mention he had a li'l girl?*"

CRIME 'N' PUNISH-MENT

CHAPTER 2

DON'T PUSH IT, BITCH! (IN CITY MARKET, SAVANNAH)

"ONE DAY SHE'S *gonna come for me.*"
I'd spent my entire childhood repeating that promise to myself, over and over, as I'd gaze up at the only image I'd ever had of my mama: a photograph in a small wooden frame that Gran'mama kept atop the windowsill in our living room. She looked so beautiful in that picture, with her pearl earrings and her hair in a bouffant twist; her glamorous face resting on the back of her left hand with its long, polished fingernails.

Mama and my daddy'd gone their separate ways after she got pregnant with me, and they'd divorced a few years after I was born and she was already living in Illinois. Aside from the occasional greeting by telephone, that photo was the only sign of Mama till the day she came home. The blemish of having a sissy child wasn't the most charming prospect she could've expected to inherit back from Gran'mama when she returned to Quincy to start a new life. From that day till I found the conviction and courage to move out six years later, all I can remember of my time with Mama was one winding and turbulent tour down the path of *misery.*

When she finally came for me, I was nine and she was pregnant; her belly almost as big as me. She wore some very *city* like maternity clothes—all in *red* from head to toe—'cause she'd worked not too far from the flagship store of Marshall Field's. Now she'd brought all of that glamorous know-how back home. 'Course, the extent of Quincy's fashion forecast was a couple pairs of Wrangler dungarees for working in the tobacco fields and a good canvas apron for slaughtering the evening's supper. Mama'd also had that uptown woman's attitude, which impressed me just as much as it scared the shit outta me.

"Maybe y'should take the child, Desia Mae. Y'can do more for him," so thought Gran'mama, who could never have imagined what kinda situation I'd really be getting into when she turned me over to her daughter. I wanted to stay put, but she thought it was best for me to go with Mama and her new hubby, Mr. John Fairley, our local dry cleaner. Y'heard right, girlfriend: Mama didn't come back alone. She had with her a new man; my four-year-old younger brother, Jerome—compliments of the ex-husband she'd left behind—and now, by her third, a baby well on the way. Hell, I still didn't even know who *she* was. (But, just so y'following this li'l soap opera, y'also need to know that Mama has two other children, both of 'em older: my sister Lois, known as Peachy-Pat, has got eleven years on me, and my sister Cynthia's got six. All of us had a different daddy for each of our last names.)

Mama practiced nursing at Sunnyland Hospital in Tallahassee, which must not have paid too well, 'cause she also ran a juke joint—a li'l bar outta which she bootlegged liquor in a county that wasn't dry for lack of rain. Her very light skinned husband had his own business, which was simply known as Fairley's Drycleaners and was located in a red-brick building shaped like a half barrel, right smack dab in the commercial district on the *colored* side of town.

I moved in with the Fairleys just round the time Mama delivered John, Jr., named for my new stepdaddy. I'd always pretended that hers were my children, 'cause I'd have to feed 'em and clean up after 'em, as well as look after the house. When Mama wasn't there, I'd also have to take care of my stepdaddy, so I'd even fantasize 'bout him being my husband, even though the sonofabitch hated my guts.

The only time my stepdaddy and I ever talked was when I worked at his store and did something wrong or when we all prayed and I'd be asked to say a Bible verse. Mostly, his sense of affection was shown by taking me to Shoney's for a burger or for a ride in his Dodge Monaco on Sundays after church. As far as hugging goes—no, none of that. I mean, two of us were his stepchildren, and him and Mama had my youngest brother, so he only had one natural child and one rightful responsibility, but he took on the raising of me and Jerome, too. And since I had a roof over my head and food to eat and clothes for school, that musta been some form of love and not just a sense of duty he showed. *At least that's what I thought.*

My own sense of duty was prob'ly connected to the extreme paranoia that I felt as a ten-year-old sissy-child, confused and insecure, whose position in all of this was never once supported by those three li'l words. I'd always figured that Jerome had it good on account of the fact that his real daddy, Mr. Charles Whiteside, had a li'l money, which he'd send to Mama on a regular basis. So Jerome was *in there* as far as a pecking order went, 'cause caring for him meant a good return on the dollar. And John, Jr.? Well, he was clearly the favorite for the simple reason that he was *blessedly* light-skinned, a physical reminder of my stepdaddy's gene pool.

No Santa Claus ever came down our chimney that I ever recall, 'cause the Fairleys never made a big commotion 'bout Christmas. We never had a tree, and there certainly wasn't any talk of Christmas *dinner*. Presents meant school clothes mostly, though I'd usually get that kinda stuff well before the holidays, so there was none of this opening-up-lotsa-gifts kinda thing. We simply observed it by going to church, treating the day for what it is, a religious holiday.

But I'll never forget one particular Christmas. I finally got up the nerve to ask Mama for a bicycle I wanted so bad, a girl's bike, the kind with no bar. I begged and begged. And it musta worked, 'cause that morning I awoke to find it miraculously displayed to the side of the kitchen table. If neither one of them had ever once told me they loved me, all of that seemed to vanish now as I drooled over the only wish that'd ever come true. I got so excited that I began sissy-squealing with delight and ran to my mama's bedroom to plant a big ol' thank-you kiss on her snoring cheek.

"Don't y'touch that bicycle," she yelled, angry at me for waking her. "Don't y'even look at it!" Mama scolded, just before she got nestled all snug in her bed, *while visions of sugar daddies danced in her head.* Two hours later she emerged in a pink night-gown-and-robe combo, marched right over to the bike, pushed the kickstand up with the spiked heel of her pom-pommed Zsa-Zsa slipper, and wheeled that li'l beauty on out to the back porch, where it remained for the next two months.

'Round February, and outta the blue, one day she came home

to find me scrubbing away at the stains on the bathroom tile and told me to go out and ride my bike like other normal boys. Oooh, child, I was ecstatic! The first thing I did was steal a couple clothespins from the neighbor's laundry tree and pin some playing cards onto the frames of the bike's wheels—y'know, so the spokes would make that flapping noise—'cause that was the thing to do back then. Then I polished up the handlebars with a mixture of ammonia and water so they'd gleam in the Quincy sunshine. My very own first bicycle was red and a two-wheeler. The banana seat didn't have the big flowers on it like I'd prayed for, but at least the seat was girls' white and not boys' black. Now she was ready! *So was the bike.*

I was riding it down the street and I crossed the intersection smiling with glee, happy to be free, and thrilled to finally get my bike after a two-month wait that coulda been longer, 'cause there was no way of predicting when Mama's moods might shift.

But damn the child who daydreams with bicycle ecstacy and then gets lost in its pleasure and never sees the sudden motion of the car she collides with! No, ma'am. If I'd been more careful on that first day, I mighta seen that dark-green flash of machinery that sideswiped my front spokes fast enough for me to be wearing that Buick's fenders like a mink stole! My one and only Christmas present was forever lost under the frame of that Riviera, but luck'ly, I didn't suffer so much as a scratch.

I'd always wanted my birthday to have the same importance as the ones celebrated on the *Mickey Mouse Club*. And so, for my eleventh birthday, the following month after the bicycle incident, *Mama* actually threw me a party! She said I could invite all the folks I wanted. Her juke joint was decorated with its usual posters of Schlitz beer and flyers announcing car washes. Mama'd also strung up a bunch of light-blue balloons and covered all the tables with matching blue paper plates and napkins and a mess of party favors, the sorta stuff she'd never have put together at home. On another table all by itself was my birthday cake: two-tier chocolate with a white icing inscription that read, "Happy Birthday Benji." A whole other table featured a heap of fried chicken and lotsa side dishes and two washbuckets filled with crushed ice and an assortment of soft drinks. My aunt Tee even made her famous grain-alcohol punch for the grown-ups.

As I looked out the window, I could see all the folks coming to celebrate *my birthday*. I'd never had a real birthday celebration before, or *any* celebration in my honor, so a party to ring in my preteen years musta seemed like the best reason of all to wait for this kinda occasion. For my birthday present, I'd asked for a record player, and—*hallelujah*—there it sat all closed up, looking like a big blue makeup case, off to the side with a big blue bow on it so everybody'd know it was *mine*.

Before my party even began, Mama told me to leave. I think I was sashaying round a bit too much or perhaps I got too sissy with excitement at seeing all these folks there just for *me*. Only minutes after everybody finished kissing and hugging me hello and wishing me many more to come, she made me go home. When I eventually got that damn record player, I barely used it, since I couldn't afford to buy any records.

Seeing as my reality mostly stunk, I guess my childhood was devoted to fantasy, 'cept for my days in school. My grades were always good. I was usually an *A* student, and whoever the prettiest teacher was, I was gonna be her pet! I'd make sure of that. It was at Stevens Elementary School, though, that I got saddled with a *mean-ass* black bitch named Miss Irene Belle. Oooh, honey, that bitch was *mean*! A li'l-bitty thing of a woman, she picked on me constantly, always asking me the toughest questions first and never once giving me the benefit of the doubt. I never understood why. I guess she musta resented the fact that I had better legs.

Luck'ly the next year, the Lord saw to it that I got myself a reprieve, 'cause I had the privilege of being taught by one of the great influences in my life, Miss Monroe, a white woman, who was the exact opposite of Miss Irene Belle. She was very large and she always smelled like Dove soap. Wore lotsa that *Avon* jewelry, too. Her voice was a velvet purr that seemed to sing soprano, even when she said, "Good morning!" Oooh, Miss Monroe was a cherub if there ever was one!

But girlfriend earned her wings and halo just on the personal attention she gave each one of her students—specially me. Miss Monroe was the first person to open the door to the white world

for me, in that she'd always make sure I was integrated with the other kids when she'd appoint me to be a class-project leader. This musta been why The Doll enjoyed school so much: she knew she'd get a chance to mix and mingle! Up till this time—which was round 1965—things were still pretty segregated throughout the state of Florida.

When I got to Quincy Junior High in the sixth grade, my love for school came to a screeching halt, thanks to a mighty run-in with one of my instructors, a man named Calvin Shearer. He taught the Future Farmers of America course, which I decided to take with a whole lotta zeal, but not 'cause I gave a rat's ass 'bout planting and tilling. No, baby, I was hitting puberty, and the Future Farmers of America was where all the *boys* were!

The lessons each week were of the raising-livestock variety, and sorta everything y'ever wanted to know 'bout fertilizer but were afraid to ask. Maybe I was too young to appreciate this fascinating information, but I found myself snickering most of the time when it got too dull—which was every minute of it—so I'd flirt a li'l to get the other boys' attention. The cuter ones could always count on my verbal and visual commentary while Mr. Calvin Shearer'd be at the blackboard, his back turned to the class, sketching out the anatomy of a rooster or something. Hearing me mimic him, our teacher'd throw me a mean-ass look and shut me up right quick, then I'd blow him a kiss and wink at all the boys. Oooh, girl, I was some kinda silly!

Well, one day, Mr. Calvin Shearer musta been real irritated by my occasional disruptions, 'cause right in the middle of a speech on swine husbandry, he marched over to my desk, looked me square in the eye, and flung down his eraser with a sharp snap. The clouds of chalk dusted the air between us. Now, Miss Benji loved herself a touch of powder, but this was too much.

"Shut the hell up, Benjamin Knox!" The boys in my class gasped and suddenly sat upright. "I don't like *homosexuals* like you!" Child, listen to me when I tell you I was some kinda stunned.

I'd never heard the word "homosexual" before—didn't know what one was—but I could tell by his disgust that he surely wasn't complimenting my Maybelline eyelashes. The whole class was mute for what seemed like the longest time, till Mr. Calvin Shearer cleared his large sewer of a throat in relief. I got so embarrassed by the pressure to utter something that wouldn't come outta my mouth, I dashed from the room in defeat.

I ran crying down the hall to see my aunt Tee, who was the English teacher at our junior high school. She immediately left her own crowded classroom to rush with me back to mine. Mr. Calvin Shearer—who knew something was up—was now standing outside, pacing like a drill sergeant.

"Just what do you mean, Calvin Shearer, calling a child, a student at our school, *to say nothing of him being my nephew,* a *filthy* and outrageous name like…?" my aunt demanded, with no less than a foot's distance between 'em. She confronted that sonofabitch with the only charitable shred of poise and dignity she was gonna let him have.

"Y'nephew was disruptin' our class…" he tried to counter, just

barely able to finish his defense when Aunt Tee ordered him to apologize—as she put it—*immediately!* Then she musta said something else to him I didn't quite hear, 'cause after this incident, I could say anything I wanted to in the Future Farmers of America! 'Course I never did have much more to say 'bout fertilizer.

Homosexual. There's something real scary 'bout the first time a gay kid hears that word. All at once it's both foreign and familiar, the answer to the mystery but still so much a jigsaw puzzle. I knew instantly that this term was some kinda murky explanation for who I really was. He used that word to silence me, and it did, all right. *I don't like homosexuals like you.* He hated the very thing that I'd just officially learned I was. What I didn't understand was why he had to say it in front of the whole class. *Why?*

My family has always been open to whatever anybody does or is—all 'cept for Mama. But the rest of 'em are pretty much all-round loving people: if y'poor, love you; if y'black, love you; if y'white, love you. I had learned enough strength from my family so that I could handle being called a name *once in a while,* though I wasn't prepared for Mr. Calvin Shearer's personal attack. And I don't think that anything the Lord or even Gran'mama'd ever preached could've prepared me for the living hell that was essentially my *domestic* existence during the years that I was part of the Fairley family.

For Mama and my stepdaddy, the shame factor of having a li'l girl with candy was too great to bear. And for this reason alone, I still assume, they took to exorcising the demon seed from my very soul with the fiercest lashings a person could possibly be capable of giving to another. Only the outside bruises have ever really healed.

"Get into the bathroom and take off y'clothes! GET BUCK NEKKID NOW! 'Cause I'm gonna whip y'colored ass!"

This was the preamble to what I received as a ritual, several times a week, for six years of my life. *What prompted it?* Nothing and everything. What*ever.* I'd stayed out too late or got an occasional *D* on my report card or cooked something from the freezer I shouldn't have or maybe I'd had one of my neighbor boyfriends over visiting when Mama wasn't home. I don't think I did anything any other child didn't do; I was just punished more severely. I never understood what I was doing wrong. But there was always something. Even if the other young'uns fucked up, *I'd* get blamed. And I'd get it. Oooh, I'd get it. For this, I hated 'em both.

I think the worst beatings came once my hormones started working and I'd be having the li'l boys over on a regular basis. That was prob'ly considered a "gay" activity by Mama's and my stepdaddy's notions, so they'd punish me, basic'ly, for what amounted to my being gay and acting on my *gayness*. Sometimes Mama caught me at her vanity playing with her makeup. And on more than a few occasions, she'd discovered that the grits mix was running low, the laundry wasn't washed good enough, or John, Jr. refused his bath. That's all she'd need to justify my slave whippings. It didn't take anything major to set her off. Sometimes just my fem'nine presence alone was enough to provoke her rage.

It was all very routine: Mama instructed what my stepdaddy performed. They'd send me first to the bathroom and make me strip. Then they'd take three long branches from a backyard oak tree that they'd braid to make a "switch" the length of a yardstick.

"Why do y'hate me? I do everythin' for y'all—why do y'hate me so much?"

The whole neighborhood could hear me screaming and hollering at 'em as they whipped the shit outta me. As the blood dripped down my ass, I'd be taken to the back porch and tied round one of them skinny beams that connected the porch to the foundation of our house. Along the way, Mama'd be swatting my head, furious that the red droplets were littering her carpet, while I limped behind in the tight grip of my stepdaddy, who was dragging me toward the porch, my body bobbing at his feet like some kinda puppet.

Tied up and alone, weak, shriveled, and sore, I'd stare up to the sky, demanding to know why a former Assistant Superintendent of the sunday school was being subjected to this nightmare, which ended only when the insects feeding off my wounds decided the banquet was over. There'd be Mama and my stepdaddy, looking out at me so solemnly from that big window in our kitchen, silently praying that maybe this time they'd *finally* made a boy outta me.

Please don't get me wrong. I love my mama to death. But back then Mama herself was young and she had her dreams, too: one of 'em surely wasn't having some flamboyant and fem'nine son. Specially her oldest. It was like a sign of failure. Her failure. But, see, in those days, y'didn't talk about gayness. If y'were queer, y'were sick and needed to seek the Lord. And John Fairley was my stepdaddy. I lived in his home and he paid the bills. If he wanted to take a switch to my hide, there was nobody or no kinda *social agency* in those mid-1960s that coulda done shit to prevent the goings-on at 312 12th Street.

We've never actually spoken of those beatings—Mama and me. But when I look at Mama sometimes and she's telling me, "I love you," I can see it in her eyes that she's trying to tell me the guilt's been eating her up all these years. When I became an adult, I finally understood that's just the way it was. She didn't know any different. She was only playing out the hand she got dealt. Just like I was.

Mama drinks now 'cause she can't forgive herself for what she did, and she knows I can't easily forget it. But, see, Mama's got a problem with *all* her children: she only speaks to one of my sisters and she's disappointed with my brothers for giving her gran'children they can't raise from a jail cell. I'm the only one outta all of 'em who respects Mama just for being her.

I s'ppose as I got older, I realized that only the future was something *I* could control. So I let go of the anger and the blame and, with the Lord's guidance, just focused on loving Mama, flaws and all. Now when she tells me how proud she is of what I've done with my life, I'm grateful, child. I don't know if it's 'cause of "The Lady Chablis" or not, but whatever it is, I know for the very first time that she really loves me.

Finally.

THE

EMPRESS'S

NEW

CLOTHES

CHAPTER 3

MISS MARLO THOMAS wasn't the only one to change her look in the fall of 1970. No, ma'am. I was *That Girlfriend* myself. Thanks to the generous help of the Reeves sisters, Miss Lois and Miss Margaret, who sandwiched me in age and lived just down the block, I first began window-dressing my own brand of fem'ninity at the age of fourteen. These were the girls who provided The Doll with a detour to her personal destiny and, ultimately, some serious access to the ladies' room.

I started cross-dressing at the age of fourteen, first as an experiment that may have been rooted in my rebellion against Mama and then, when I built up my wardrobe, just as a matter of course. Miss Lois and Miss Margaret were very *fashionable*, given their ages and their means, and they'd gladly hand down any items of interest they no longer wore—like maybe a maxi-coat or a midi-length vest that matched a pair of hot pants. They also gave me lotsa them mid-thigh pleated skirts to wear with a blouse and knee socks—a look respectable enough for church.

Initially, my change was something I wanted to play with privately. I'd hidden my things in the back of the closet, taking 'em out ceremoniously when I'd get home from school and returning 'em just as Mama pulled into the driveway. Even if she did confiscate a few of my better dresses, I could always rely on the Reeves sisters to supply me with something else. But I also wanted to indulge my journey to the other side a helluva lot more often than I was allowed by the hours in my day.

So when I finally got up the nerve to attend school in my li'l-girl pantsuits with a fringed-and-beaded handbag in tow, I discovered, to my ever-loving surprise, that most of the teachers actually liked my look.

"Come here, y'*gotta* see Benji." They ooohed and aaahed to one another, smiling and shaking their heads in amusement, maybe even attempting to hold back a giggle. But I knew down deep they weren't really laughing at me. They were merely marveling at my bravado, even if it public'ly reinforced what Mr. Calvin Shearer'd already announced.

"Oh, y'look so good, *so natural*," my teachers might say. Let it be known, child, that none of 'em ever sent me to the principal's office for the way I was dressed, not even once. And believe me, girl, after Miss Lois relaxed my hair from an afro to a pageboy and Miss Margaret taught me how to use mascara, they had every reason to. But a year later or so, not even their compliments could make me wanna stay in school. Lipstick became my full-time refuge. I began skipping classes on a regular basis just so I could practice applying my makeup. See, I was depressed most of the time, 'cause I wanted to make my fem'ninity fully visible, which I couldn't really do in front of Mama and my stepdaddy—'less, of course, I also wanted to be buried in one of my new outfits.

The day I received my last beating, Mama'd left work early and arrived home to find me in full drag, drinking my stepdaddy's beer and entertaining the boys from next door right in the middle of our living room. I remember pleading with her to stop, and I screamed from the basement of my lungs. But nothing could arrest her rage at finding her son in a dress and the Clarence boys in her house when she wasn't home. She could see by the dirty plates on our coffee table that I'd fed 'em whatever leftovers we'd still had in the fridge. I'm sure she also guessed at what I'd served 'em for dessert.

My sister Cynthia took me in for a while after I'd arrived at her door, a blood-soaked transvestite-in-training and the worse for wear from my crosstown sprint. I told her 'bout the abuse. All six years' worth. She was as sympathetic as she could be, considering that there wasn't gonna be any more financial aid from Mama, which left me with a couple weeks of their hospitality to figure out my next move.

Not far from where I'd lived with Mama was a whole complex of low-income apartments—*the projects*—which were separated from downtown Quincy by a bunch of woods. There were all these trails that led back and forth to downtown, so folks'd be walking these li'l paths constantly. A tiny pedestrian bridge sat over the same creek that streamed down from Gran'mama's place. On the many days I began playing hookey, I'd sit at this bridge, contemplating my situation while I painted my toenails and lighted up the cigarettes I'd recently taught myself to smoke. That's when Connie came by.

She didn't know me, really, 'cept she knew that I was Desia Mae's child. On this particular day, when I noticed her standing above me, I guess I was crying.

"What's wrong with you, child?" Connie asked, squatting down some on her big ol' backside to face me at eye level.

"It's Mama. I can't take it no more. They done whipped my ass for the very last time! I ain't ever goin' back!" I said as I rolled up my pink tank top to display the speckled imprints from Mama's heels that still remained on my upper back.

"Y'wanna come live with me, baby? I'll handle y'mama."

Oooh, girl, could it be? This was like some answered prayer. But I still couldn't believe it was true. Sure enough, though, Connie took me back to her place and called Mama.

"Benji's gonna come stay with me for a while, Desia Mae," she said without even asking permission. Mama knew I wanted to leave for good, and she knew it was prob'ly best: I *was* getting very rebellious—what with my new wardrobe and all—and she didn't know how to handle it. Connie, on the other hand, didn't seem to care that I was gay. From that day on, she supported me in every way. She became the mother I'd always wished I'd had.

This particular time in my life gave me the advantages of freedom I could never have experienced when I lived with Mama, and certainly not when I lived with Gran'mama. Connie herself was carefree and independent. Close to forty, she'd been married once, then separated, and she'd had several miscarriages, which she said she'd mourned till the day *I* entered her life. She never let me once forget that I turned out to be the child she'd long hoped to name. So I took "Chablis" with her blessing and gratitude, and told her I'd find a good use for it someday.

Connie was a gospel singer when I went to live with her. Singing for the Lord made her happiest, but she didn't live her life according to the Book. She'd made her own rules, and she expected others to do the same. A voluptuous size 18 with a flirtatious walk, she was known throughout the projects for her wicked sense of humor and a voice as rich as the late, great Mahalia Jackson.

I wasn't working or going to school, but Connie'd give me some pocket money whenever she could. Whatever she had, she shared. See, Connie was being "kept," if y'wanna call it that, by an older, married man who sang with her in church. While he also supported a family of five, he made sure that we had a stocked fridge and free rent. And I made sure to leave 'em both in peace on the Wednesday nights when he'd come to call.

But Connie never once told me to look for a job. I was her child, her *daughter*, her responsibility, and that's how she treated me. She'd often show me affection and encouragement with a spontaneous hug or a rub of the shoulder. Not once did she gimme an ounce of negativity; it was always positive. Even when I did something wrong, she'd explain it to me, not try and beat it outta me. It was kinda like being back with Gran'mama—only Connie moisturized *her own* scalp.

I realized right then what a *true* mama's s'pposed to be. Every morning, she'd get up from the sofa she sometimes snoozed the night on, pull herself together with the aid of a kerchief and a floral housecoat, and have my breakfast spread across the table of her tiny kitchen. She even took a small spare room where she'd kept her storage and, with the help of some neighbor friends, moved everything out to make it mine.

"This is y'room, Benji. When y'need to be alone, y'come in here and close the door." Gosh, she made me feel like I'd won the lottery.

Girl, my very first bedroom was soon-to-be painted baby blue, which I chose 'cause I figured it was the color of heaven. There were two white throw rugs and lotsa colorful pillows and stuffed animals all round to make the place extra cute and fem'nine. Just like The Doll. Gran'mama'd even made me a quilt to match the color scheme. And Connie taught me how to organize my closet so I had all my pretty stuff *on display* and all my boy clothes— which were thankfully dwindling—hid *way* outta sight. I had one album, *Make It Easy on Yourself,* that I placed over the white bureau Connie'd found at the Goodwill. I wanted to imagine that it was Miss Dionne Warwick's—or any beautiful woman's—face I saw when I looked in the mirror.

But while I'd be free to dress up as I pleased, *whenever I pleased,* I did keep a reserve suit and tie in my closet to wear to church with Connie. I'd never go to church dressed as a girl. At least not yet. It was outta respect for Jesus Christ. I figured He was already doing all He could to help the cause.

Besides, Quincy was a small town to begin with, and as it was, I'd already pushed it to the limit. I wasn't gonna go to church all dressed up, only to have the people who *didn't* give a damn what I was doing think that I somehow disrespected God. That woulda been a li'l too much even in an era of gay liberation. Nowadays, of course, I don't hesitate to be me in the house of the Lord, but back then I was still reconciling who I was.

'Course, outside of church, y'mama was *ready!* I'd always be wearing my earrings and carrying my purse and wearing my jumpsuit and my li'l *fish* shoes. That's often how you'd have seen The Doll combing the boulevards of Quincy! If Mama happened to drive by while I was *strolling,* I didn't give a shit. I'd already stopped going over to her house, so if she knew 'bout me, it was usually by word of mouth or it was 'cause she'd spotted me when she'd cruise round town in her big ol' Bonneville sedan.

On my journey to self-awareness, I'd begun hanging out with this one girl named Rhonda Conyers, who eventually became my first real female mentor. She lived directly across the street from where I lived in the projects with Connie. Miss Rhond, as I called her, had to be at least eight years older than me. She was black, but she had the chiseled facial features and thick straight tresses of a white girl. She'd even had her nose pierced and it was still only the early seventies. Mostly, she was some kinda *sexyyy*—on the order of Miss Janet Jackson herself, if y'will. Miss Rhond had a perfect shape, a plunging cleavage, and a raspy voice as a result of all that reefer she smoked. Though she lived off welfare and food stamps, she managed to pull together the most amazing fashion creations from the Salvation Army. It was dazzling. The girl's style was known to one and all, and she passed those beauty secrets on to me. Oooh, she was the hottest thing in that city, honey!

What I loved most 'bout Miss Rhond was that she always made me feel *genuine*. She never once referred to me as a "him" or called me a boy. She acknowledged me for the woman I was becoming, and she gladly coached me in the many ways a gal withholds her mystery when she's planning a good seduction. Thanks to Miss Rhond, my ample assortment of women's clothes—dresses, stockings, shoes, y'name it—were coming on strong, and almost everybody from the projects was donating something to my cause for womanhood. Yes, girl, it was Miss Rhond who'd engineered my li'l clothing drive, which, I might add, never cost y'mama a red cent.

Every morning, she'd open up her front door and yell, "Miss Benji. Miss Benji. *Miss Pee-Wee.*" Yeah, the folks round town began calling me that 'cause I was so petite and also 'cause it was more—what we'd say today—*androgynous* or gender neutral than Benji or even Miss Benji was. The sound of Miss Rhond's voice signaled the start of a new day's escapades. I'd tell Connie I was off to class, and on some days, that was certainly no lie. But increasingly, I'd make a beeline instead for the home of Miss Rhonda Conyers.

She had a room in her li'l apartment with nothing but huge pillows to lounge on, soul posters all round, and this one black light we'd turn on only as a kinda *mood* ritual before we got high. It was here in this room where we'd be discussing the boys we fancied and hatching our plans to lure 'em in. Miss Rhond loved her reefer and she loved hard liquor, *and she introduced me to both*. Sometimes we'd lie back on them pillows and pass a joint in silence—that black light on and nothing else, 'cept sometimes the music of Ike and Tina, rolling us on the river to nowhere. Other times it was Jimi Hendrix blasting away on Miss Rhonda Conyers's ol' hi-fi. It mighta been ten A.M. outside, but inside the idea of time was of no consequence to a couple of white chicks sitting round talking. This was Miss Pee-Wee's Playhouse, a room that became a shrine to my *maturing* process, where I could explore myself without explanation.

Needless to say, I was losing scholastic interest some kinda fast. See, I wanted *adult*hood, 'cause what I was now tasting of it was way better than anything I knew up till then. After the torture of my living my older childhood years with Mama, my teen years with Miss Rhonda Conyers was gonna be my time to relax. At least that's what I'd intended when I flirted with dropping outta school for a while.

I was in the ninth grade when I moved in with Connie, but my grades were going down as reliably as The Doll's been known to do on a blind date. It hurt Connie to see me give up in my sophomore year, but she couldn't force me to go, 'cause I was gonna go anywhere else *but* school, and she knew it. She'd always tried to stress how important it was that I finish my education, but she left the decision up to me. Ultimately, I chose to leave.

Round this time, now, I was also getting involved with a guy named Sammy Green. He was my age, and we'd gone to school together all my life. He had big ol' lips, a big ol' afro, and, best of all, a big ol' box, which I had a hard time keeping my eyes off of. He played drums in a popular blues band, and I became his biggest groupie. He'd call on me at Miss Pee-Wee's Playhouse, or we'd leave Miss Rhond with a li'l privacy and go a-ridin' in the car he drove *illegally.* 'Cause at the age of fifteen, he was too young for even a learner's permit, according to the state of Florida in 1972.

Well, after Sammy came Larry Marks. No, actually, Larry Marks came before Sammy, if y'wanna get technical. *Okay,* so Larry Marks was my first semi-boyfriend/crush thing. I'd also known him from grade school, and as kids, we'd often spent the weekends at his folks' house, since the Fairleys were never inclined to let me entertain. Every time I'd slept with him in his bed, we'd make the earth move. In fact, Larry Marks was the one who first taught me how to masturbate. As we got older, in our teens, and I'd left Mama to live with Connie, we were still seeing each other, even though I was also seeing Sammy on the side.

Larry was also in a band, known as the Untouchables, and unlike Sammy's, which was mostly a small group of boys who gathered in a garage to make music, Larry's band actually crossed the state border to play their gigs. Since I wasn't doing any homework, I'd often travel with him to nearby towns like Valdosta and Bainbridge, Georgia, just to get out and party.

The Untouchables accepted me and treated me like a girl,

'cause I looked like any other girl one of 'em might be dating. I never worried none about "passing." The kindly folks in Quincy already knew who and what I was, and they accepted me as Miss Benji or Miss Pee-Wee without any real degree of fanfare. While I wasn't exactly stuffing my bra, I did work my God-given illusions to the max. And enhanced now by the magic of Miss Rhonda Conyers, my cosmetic transition was all but complete. Whether it was a midriff and cutoffs or strippy-strappy sandals and rayon evening pajamas, there was no question that The Doll was coming of age just in time for her sixteenth birthday.

MISS

PEE-WEE'S

BIG

ADVENTURE

CHAPTER 4

I'M GONNA ROLL ALL OVER YOU.

AT SWEET SIXTEEN, just being me meant lotsa solitary hours figuring out how to resolve what I felt was right 'bout myself, so that it could be understood and accepted by folks who tried to tell me otherwise. I *was* different from most other members of my natural sex: I was born a woman, and not till I could reconcile my true identity with what my family or society expected of me, could I ever fit into something that looked like the all-American dream.

But credit The Doll for being the resourceful li'l mistress of self-promotion that she is. 'Cause she educated the good folks of Quincy, Florida, who'd begun to accept her visible fem'ninity, at least, and even appreciate what it was that made her so captivatingly different. No, I was *not* something they'd ever seen before, but I was perceived as a girl 'cause I carried myself like one. And if I was ever regarded as an oddity, I was also a damn sure *likable* one! Hell, even a local elected official acquired himself a taste for Miss Thang.

This official first made my acquaintance when I'd sometimes assisted Mama with the bootlegging business she operated outta the back of her Bonneville in the parking lot of the juke joint she used as a cover. Hers only had a beer and wine license, 'cause that's all she could legally sell in a dry county like Quincy's. The stronger stuff she'd pick up in Tallahassee, where, you'll recall, she did her nursing.

I'd spent many of my Saturday nights when I was ten and eleven helping her out, so that she'd wouldn't be seen leaving the premises—which mighta been too conspicuous, see, since she was basic'ly breaking the law. It was my job to wait at her side for the first customer who'd ask for a half pint. Then, I'd be sent to the trunk of her car to grab some gin or whiskey—whatever she'd found on sale—and stuff it into my pants to sneak back inside, where I'd pass it to Mama, who'd wait to get paid before she poured the full contents of the bottle into a tall plastic cup or two. Then she'd hand me back the empty to smash out back in a li'l box we used for destroying the evidence. Y'got all of that?

I was always providing the booze run for Quincy's Finest, 'cause they was Mama's best customers. So Mr. Official knew I was Desia's child, the underage accomplice who made his sleepy Saturday night just a li'l more tolerable. Six years later and nothing had changed, really, 'cause I was still much obliged when it came to serving our local politician.

He was a tall, older white guy in his forties—grayish wavy hair and a very attractive, rugged kinda face and body, like you'd expect to see on any southern state patrolman in a Miss Burt Reynolds movie. But he wasn't looking for a pint of gin when he'd see me strutting round the streets of Quincy, courteously offering me a ride to the destination of my choice whenever he was not working and *happened* to spot me. No, ma'am. I was beginning to think he had himself some E.S.P. And I know for a fact he had himself some D.O.L.L.

He liked to take her to this secluded li'l lake, where he took his time in the seduction department, savoring the supple softness of her legs and the upper landscape of a shaven forest he never saw for the tree he was more eager to climb.

In exchange for each of these "sessions"—he used this as a code word between us—he'd gimme ten bucks or a carton of Winstons, which weren't my mentholated brand but didn't seem like anything to sneeze at when I didn't have an income. He didn't even have to fear my screaming to Mama with tales of molestation, 'cause I'd already been moved out a year. 'Course, he didn't need to know that neither.

But apart from my privacy, I also wanted this official as a repeat customer, so it wouldn't have behooved me to open my mouth to anyone but his—*him,* I mean. And besides, all modesty aside, I was also juggling the favors of a married preacher from Connie's church—the Reverend Felix Munson—who often fancied a li'l *communion* just after Sunday services. Amen to that, child.

And nice work if y'can get it.

These were the folks who taught me about grown-up physical expression when I decided who and what I was gonna be. The Doll was something they definitely knew they wanted. And she was delighted to feel needed. Looking back, this was not *abuse* in any way, as I see it, but a very consensual learning experience that occurred for a couple years during the prime of my burgeoning girlhood.

Now, 'less y'think I was something of a harlot, let it be known here and now that I never actually had intercourse with anyone till I was twenty-one. What I enjoyed as a teenager was a kind of physical exploration. Plain and simple.

Since I was a *bit* of a vixen-in-training, though, I was also known for the occasional lapse of judgment with the law. Mostly, I'd get caught drinking underage in a bar. But another time it was something in the neighborhood of petty theft.

My first significant bit of *grand* larceny was not without a *judicial* consequence. Miss Rhonda Conyers had just pierced my ears with a needle from Connie's sewing kit, and I couldn't go round wearing them silver training studs forever, since they went with so few of my outfits. I needed to sparkle. But I also needed a job. So what's a girl to do when she hasn't made a penny lately off her trips to the powder room? She trots on over to the Belk department store and steals herself a big, fat pair of gold hoops like the kind on Cleopatra Jones in the movies. Only she hopes she don't get caught.

"Oooh, I like these here earrin's," I said to Miss Mary Ann Dillon, who was along for this heist on account of her notorious stealing skills. "Take 'em," was her only response. We'd combed all four sides of the costume-jewelry counter, looking for just the right pair to grace my subtle features. I pulled our mark gently off the sales tree and looked round carefully to see if the coast was clear. Miss Mary Ann distracted the only salesgirl I noticed in the vicinity with some sorta question 'bout Lipsmackers just as I opened my purse to give my new earrings a free fall.

Now, I may've been prettier than Miss Mary Ann Dillon, but as a shoplifter I came in sorry-ass second. If this'd been *her* operation, she'd have also checked for the salesgirl at the adjacent *handbags* counter.

My *criminal* stage was over in a flash, as Belk security cornered me, snatched my macramé purse, and retrieved them new earrings while the salesgirl called the police. My only impulse was to call Gran'mama, who was forced to leave her work at the Ashleys' place and hightail her Plymouth Valiant over to the juvenile court—in the very cellar of that big, beautiful building right in the heart of downtown Quincy.

"You can accept the release of this child as your responsibility, or you can place this child in the custody of the county jail for thirty days," the judge offered Gran'mama, who bravely held back her emotions in order to make a sane decision.

Now, The Doll's made some mistakes in her life, child. However, she's never been sorrier than the day she'd watched her sweet, loving gran'mama agonize public'ly over the torment and shame that it cost her to tell that rotten judge to leave my ass right where it was. And not *once* did Gran'mama ever come visit me. I'd exposed her own law-abiding soul to so much disgrace, she didn't even send a letter. She wanted to teach me a lesson, and it was a lesson well-learned. I never wanted to hurt Gran'mama, and I vowed I would never steal again.

Jail wasn't so bad. While the legal system treated me like a guy, my fellow inmates sure didn't. Before my stretch here, I never knew if my allure was mostly on account of my best friendship with Miss Rhonda Conyers or if I'd had some fashion sense of my own. I mean, I couldn't do my makeup here, so I had to be enterprising and rely on my flawless cheekbones. (You'd also be interested to know that a standard-issue T-shirt instantly becomes a halter if y'pull the front side over to the back of y'neck!)

My protector and provider at the Quincy jail was this older man named Clyde Waters, whose blue-collar brawn reminded me of the father on *Good Times*. He was there when I got there and still there when I left. He was 'bout sixty, and he had some setup with the system where he could go off to his job as a landscaper and return to his cell like it was a suite at the Ramada. I didn't care what his deal was, 'cause I'd quickly become the sole beneficiary of any stuff I'd ask him to bring me from outside—cigarettes, mostly, but also some notes from Miss Rhond and Connie and even the occasional joint. I guess I musta felt a li'l *beholden* to him for wanting nothing in return.

After twenty-five days, I was released early for good behavior. Just in the nick of time, girl! These men weren't imprisoned by the system alone. Their desire for The Doll was also doing time. So I said "See ya!" to all this caged heat—with a stream of waves, whistles, and cheers flying past—and I sashayed down that cell-to-cell runway like Miss Naomi Campbell for Chanel!

"*Bye, bye,* Miss Benji," yelled one of my admirers.

"Go on, *Pee-Wee!*" barked somebody else.

"When I get out, I'm gonna look y'up, so don't act like y'don't know me, now!" shot another. I blew *him* a kiss.

Returning to Connie's just in time for the Christmas holidays, I recounted my prison escapades to both her amusement and dismay. As usual, Connie didn't really judge me. She just spoke briefly 'bout how she'd hoped I'd learned a valuable lesson and all of that and then joked that Santa was prob'ly gonna leave coal in my stocking. Across the way, Miss Rhonda Conyers—who faithfully visited all three weeks—was waiting on me impatiently. And down the next building over, so was Greg Landon.

During my stay with Connie, I had me a mild fling with this man, who had himself a wicked li'l crush on The Doll. Problem was he also had a wife and three children. I'd made a rule only to see him 'bout every other weekend—or whenever it was he got paid—'cause it ate up my conscience to be laying up too often with someone else's husband. He'd usually locate me at Miss Rhond's as soon as he cashed his check, and we'd go a-ridin' through the backstreets of Quincy before we'd park the car for a li'l prelude drink and smoke. If I felt up to it, we'd head on into the woods, throw down a blanket, and y'know the rest.

I guess I was turning into a bit of a scandal, one whose life was becoming a big, bad soap opera filled with consecutive episodes of mischief and disgrace. And since I wasn't going to school none, I'd hang out nightly, getting drunk at the juke joints.

These places were mostly back in the woods, places y'knew how to find if y'were part of the black community, 'cause those were the folks these li'l clubs were run for. Back in the woods, there'd be no neighbors or traffic, see, so the police knew what y'were doing, but y'could do it 'cause y'were hiding out. The Patio was the particular favorite of Miss Rhonda Conyers and The Doll. It was a ratty place that y'passed through a swinging glass door to enter. Booths all round. And a huge ol' jukebox along the very back wall was where y'played y'music, and played it loud. In a nice li'l *unisex* twist that I didn't mind a bit, there was only one bathroom, though I mostly used the side of the building myself.

Miss Rhonda Conyers and me'd hang out at the Patio at least three times a week, flirt some and get piss-drunk off a bottle of Boone's Farm Candy Apple Red wine that was usually on special. I drank so much that one night I passed out on one of the booths in the back. And as Miss Lady Luck would have it, my cousin Bosco—bless his soul—saw me there and had to pull my ass outta the joint to save our family's reputation.

Bosco was Aunt Katie Bell's son. He's long dead now (*murdered*, though I ain't quite sure of the facts), but he was about four or five years older than me, and, girl, he was one of my relatives I woulda *gave* some to. He was just *so-o-o* fine. He also had the heart of his mama and a responsible instinct that didn't seem to come with my set of chromosomes. Now, Cousin Bosco didn't have a problem with my girlishness—just my acting like a boozing hussy.

I never was one to really hold my alcohol very well. So I decided to sprawl out on the seat of the booth. Cousin Bosco tried several times to rouse me, and I wouldn't or I'd just mumble something stupid. When he finally got y'mama to stand, her gelatin legs gave way to a quick stumble before she swan-dived facedown on the Formica. My brave and handsome cousin lifted The Doll over his shoulder like he was Tarzan and removed her drunken, embarrassed ass from the bar. Then he took her to the back of the building and threw her in the Dumpster!

From that day on, I learned how to handle myself. But that's when I knew, too, that I had to get outta Quincy. I could see what I was gonna become if I stayed. And the proof of that theory was realized some ten years later when I went home to see my family and dropped in on Miss Rhond. I knocked on the door—the same one in the projects where I'd left her—and she peered out like some kinda scared rabbit.

"Hey, girl!" I said, all happy to be reunited with the first bitch who'd taught me the meaning of rebellion.

"Is that you, Miss Pee-Wee?" She seemed kinda spooked.

"How are you?" I asked, smiling widely.

"Fine." But she sure didn't sound like she believed herself. She wouldn't even open the door. And she looked horrible. I could tell she was on crack, and I'm sure she was an alcoholic, too. She never outgrew the meaningless lifestyle we'd once had, and she was all the worse for the wear. It was heartbreaking. Whatever we once shared, it ended right there, child. She wasn't my girl no more.

I also knew while I was still in Quincy that there was more to the world than the juke joints of that Florida town. I got to be friendly with this one guy named Donny, who was a nurse, and even though nobody'd ever said it, they knew he was a big ol' sissy. He'd often come and pick me up from Connie's and take me to Tallahassee for the night. I guess he was trying to show me, best he could, that there *was* more to life for gay people than the comfort of a stiff drink.

One night, he took me to the campus of Florida A&M University, where the Alvin Ailey American Dance Theater was performing. Lord, this spectacle was like nothing I'd ever seen! I thought, God, that's what I wanna do, right there.

I turned to Donny with my naive impression of it all. "I can do that if somebody'd show me how!"

"Well, finish school and become a dancer," he suggested.

Donny was flamboyant and fun, but he also had some very sobering attitudes toward life. I was impressed with him, not just for exposing me to Alvin Ailey, but for waking up my ability to dream.

When the performance was over, Donny took me backstage and introduced me to one of the principal dancers, a handsome black guy who'd looked almost as good as The Doll does in a pair of tights. He was a friend of Donny's, and he was masculine and openly gay. So was his boyfriend. "What's *that* all 'bout," I gushed.

When I went back to Quincy with those beautiful, precious memories of that performance and of the dancer and his boyfriend we met, I was convinced my life could only get better if I got the hell outta town and did my mingling elsewhere.

I was also getting kinda restless staying with Connie, but it wouldn't be the last I'd ever see of her. We'd discover ourselves a few years later living in Atlanta, where Connie eventually got all up in the Pentecostal ministry. I'm sad to say that her pursuit of religion was the beginning of our end. See, she's a preacher now, and she's unhappy 'bout the way I've chosen to live my life. She condemns the very thing she once encouraged. We can't even talk about the past, 'cause she don't ever wanna be reminded. So I've avoided her. But I know I gotta face her at some point, if only to thank her for saving my life.

After I left Connie's, I moved to Tallahassee to live with Aunt Katie Bell for about a year and a half, when I was sixteen and seventeen. She'd always said she'd have a room for me whenever I wanted it. But these were not prosperous times for any of us, so living with Aunt Kate in a double-wide trailer wasn't exactly the Waldorf-Astoria. The loss of Cousin Bosco, her only child, had sent her to the bottle, and Uncle Lonnie'd always been a big-time drunk himself. He worked hard at his job as a machinist, but as soon as he got home, he'd head for that whiskey and two hours later, he'd be out cold. Since Aunt Kate enforced few restrictions, I mostly came and went as I pleased.

I took off to Miami one weekend with this black girl, DeeDee, who I'd met at a straight club in Tallahassee. She was a real sweet and innocent cheerleader kinda gal, with a beautiful smile and flawless teeth like Vanna White's. She wasn't a slut or a whore or nothing like that, just bisexual. DeeDee was a student at Florida A&M, and she was driving home to Miami to house-sit for her folks and asked me to ride along with her in her Volkswagen Bug—a 1965 convertible in navy blue—which she also taught me how to drive. It had a stick shift, and I'd never handled one of those.

The first night there, we went to one of them big ol' black discos—a place called the Jetaway—and I found myself caught up with the wrong kinda folks. I'd prob'ly cruised the bar twice before I'd found myself this guy, who'd said something 'bout himself being an ex-football player. What a coincidence, since I'd played a pretty good *tight end* myself. I told DeeDee I'd catch up with her at home and went off a-ridin' in his Barracuda convertible. Oooh, he was fine, showed me the moon over Miami and the stars in his eyes. So I invited him back to DeeDee's. She'd picked herself up a security guard for Burdine's department store in the meantime.

But I got a li'l carried away with this boy, and I musta forgot that I wasn't as much of a woman as I'd said, 'cause it took all of ten minutes before his large, roaming hands intercepted his gun and pointed it to my head.

"Y'tricked me, nigger," he growled.

"Y'didn't have to come here!" I spoke defiantly.

"Shut the fuck up!" he yelled loud enough to disturb DeeDee and her friend in the next room, who suddenly busted in like the FBI, except that they were naked, and not much help against a man with a gun.

My being the First Lady, I knew it was up to me to make the peace—and fast.

"Child, if you want to shoot me and go to prison for murder, then do it now, because I'm about to die from a heart attack anyway." (Thankfully, on those *rare* occasions when The Doll can't charm a man with her beauty, she can still disarm him with her wit.)

He lemme go, looking some kinda angry and embarrassed. Putting away his gun, he warned me fiercely not to hide my T like that again, saying that next time I might not be so lucky. Then he grabbed up his things and peeled on outta there, just as the sun was coming up.

I stayed awake sweating and shaking in DeeDee's arms, rethinking my strategy for picking up strangers. Girl, I knew this much was true: unless I wanted a dream date with the county coroner, I could never risk denying my candy again.

So when I got back to Tallahassee, I restricted myself to the

safety of the gay clubs, and hanging with these two femme lesbians, Renee and Carolyn, who lived in the same trailer park as my aunt. Believe it or not, I was seventeen before I'd ever been to a gay club. But these gals took me to my first—the Fox Trot—which was where I met the person whose impact on my future would rival what Gran'mama and Connie'd done for my past.

His real name was Cliff Taylor, but I'd soon come to know him better as Miss Tina Devore.

SOUTHERN

COMFORT

CHAPTER 5

Y'GOTTA FIGURE that every drag queen has a drag mother—that's just the nature of *all* things, right? A good *drag* mama is someone who launches her drag *offspring* on the road to their careers—y'know, advising and counseling and showing them how to perfect their performances and personas.

I'd known a few sissies besides me in Quincy, but Cliff Taylor was the first guy I'd ever met who also dressed up. I was totally amazed 'cause when I first laid eyes on the boy—brawny and chiseled like a black G.I. Joe—I must say I felt the biggest crush coming over me. And then I'd come to find out he was also a big ol' drag queen by the name of *Tina Devore*! Girl, it was too much to handle. I wanna make it clear that Miss Tina's male-to-female transition occurs only at night—that is, she dresses up for professional reasons only. She ain't hiding any transvestite fetishes up under them gowns of hers.

Miss Tina Devore is prob'ly 'bout seven years older than me, but she was really just getting started herself as a drag entertainer when we met. She knew all 'bout this performance art, 'cause she'd been to the gay bars in Orlando and Jacksonville and then brought it all back to Tallahassee. There was nothing till Miss Tina got things rolling. I'd never even heard of drag myself.

I began hanging with Miss Tina any chance I could. She could sense my fascination with performing in a skirt, so she introduced me to the idea that I might also have what it took to perform on stage, that is, if I'd be willing to learn the ropes. Hell, girl—unemployed and meeting each new day with a hangover, I wasn't exactly *career-driven*, now, was I?

For my first-ever drag act at the Fox Trot in Tallahassee, I wore a skanky li'l 1970s outfit: hot pants and thigh-high boots and a rayon blouse with a maxi-vest, an ensemble which Miss Tina helped me create outta my hand-me-down inheritance from the

Reeves sisters. I wasn't sure yet how I was gonna coordinate my moves with the lyrics of the song, so I went out on stage and danced like I did when it was for pleasure. Only this time I'd face the audience every few bars and move my lips.

I was almost eighteen round this time, and Miss Tina was in school at Florida State University studying drama. One day in her junior year she up and decided to move to Atlanta. She reckoned that she'd had all the schooling she'd needed, since *her* drag career'd really begun to heat up. On one of her return trips to Tallahassee, she offered to let me stay with her if I ever considered moving to Georgia.

"And if y'ever want to make something of y'life and y'career, y'gotta leave here, girl. 'Cause if y'stay, y'gonna end up bein' a wino and a barfly," she said, warning me as soberly as Nurse Donny'd done at the Alvin Ailey production. Hearing this warning the second time round, I realized Miss Tina was right. I went to Aunt Kate and told her flat out that it was time for me to get a move on—just as it had been when I'd left Connie behind in Quincy.

"If anything happens, y'always got a place to come back to," Aunt Katie Bell assured, giving me her blessing and all the security I needed to start a new life. She kissed me and pushed a few dollars into my hand. Her only other child was leaving the nest forever.

I got into Miss Tina's li'l yellow Pinto, and off we drove to Atlanta. I remember my first glimpse of the skyline in 1974 was like I was seeing Oz. Emerald City. The Peachtree City. Very pretty and some kinda fantastic. Clean and *modern*. Hell, every city should look this good after a fire!

Miss Tina had herself an apartment in midtown Atlanta, back when midtown was nothing but a string of gay bars. She also had a boyfriend—a young guy, 'bout seventeen himself, named Randy. Tall, with straight stringy hair and big hands, he was cute in a male-hustler sorta way, and he worked as a bar-backup person at the Onyx, the club where Miss Tina was working as a headliner. We all shared the place, but since the lease was in Miss Tina's name, everything was her responsibility. As generous as she was, not charging me till I got on my feet, I still had to come up with some way to earn a living.

Well, seeing as I was still unemployed, I got to know a lotta the other folks who lived in our apartment complex. Many of 'em were gay and worked nights in the bars. But in the case of these two black girls, Sabrina and Katrina, they just happened to be prostitutes, both of 'em from Mississippi. They'd go out every evening, strolling up and down Peachtree Street, the main strip in Atlanta, and pick up wealthy johns, who mostly treated 'em right. So I figured—hey, easy money. Why, I even had myself a career wardrobe to get started with.

"Y'just follow our lead and do whatever we do," they instructed. We stood at one corner, pacing and circling one another. The key to it is that y'don't wanna be seen hanging in a pack, but y'gotta stand close enough to smoke and chat while y'wait for a john to cruise by.

As cars slowed to the curb, I saw each of 'em do their thing: flirt with the driver some, then lay down the terms, then hop in and be back minutes later with cold, hard cash in their purse. I guess I waited for 'bout an hour before it was my turn to try it. A middle-aged man in a white Lincoln Continental drove up, and after a quick negotiation, I got in. He looked like somebody's school principal: bald and some kinda blind, wearing them thick gray-and-clear-colored glasses that older men still wear.

We prob'ly hadn't even turned the block when I looked over at the statuette of the Virgin Mary on his dashboard and began weeping. I guess it dawned on me right then just how sleazy the whole procedure seemed. Specially if the Blessed Mother was gonna be taking in the view!

After my one-and-only stint as The Unhappy Hooker, I cried poverty to Miss Tina, 'cause I'd run out of Aunt Kate's kindness and I couldn't come up with any more money to pay my fair share. Miss Tina understood, but suggested another option. She thought I should do the upcoming talent show at the Onyx. Hell, girl, I had nothing to lose and everything to gain, as I figured. They were giving away, I think, fifty bucks, too. For my performance number, I sang Melba Moore's "This Is It," and, yes, child, The Doll took home the first of her four crowns.

So now, as a result of my victory, the Onyx asked me to do the cameo spots once or twice a month, and lotsa new folks started coming in to see me, tipping me twenty dollars each performance and even bringing me dresses! A girl could get spoiled under these conditions. I did.

Then, to my everlasting surprise, Miss Tina and her cast from the Onyx sponsored me in another contest, which was known throughout Atlanta as Miss Chez Cabaret. They put my clothes together, did my makeup, and this time I sang Natalie Cole's "This Will Be," against the likes of some ten other contestants, all of 'em as pretty as me. This was my first *professional* contest, but I wasn't really nervous, 'cause I was so excited *and honored* 'bout participating so soon in my career. Yeah, y'guessed it, I snagged this one, too.

Afterward, an Atlanta gay magazine took my photograph and published it with a li'l blurb 'bout me winning this title. Yeah, bitch, the new Miss Chez Cabaret 1975 was Miss Pee-Wee Chablis. My first honor and my first publicity clipping. It also made the Onyx take notice, 'cause they hired me as a regular cast member for thirty-five dollars a night, plus tips, working weekly, Wednesdays through Sundays. I'd already decided my stage name was gonna be Chablis, thanks to Connie, and Miss Tina put a twist herself on that name when she brought me onto the Onyx stage for the very first time as a regular.

"Ladies and gentleman, welcome to the stage the sparklin' personality of the bubblin' *Lady* Chablis." That's exactly how she said it, and that was my first introduction with that name. Yeah, some people might make fun of it—Chablis? Oh, that's cheap wine. But I'm sorry, just listen to it: *The Lady Chablis*. I think it just *sings*!

We had many faithful customers who came to see us regularly, but Jim Nally, the owner of the Onyx, was this very bigoted white man. *Oooh, that motherfuckin' honky was pre-ju-diced!* He'd constantly get mad at us over nothing and call us all niggers. Even the white girls. Now, y'can call me a nigger 'cause I'm cute and y'crowd loves me, but above all, y'can call me a nigger *'cause I need this job!* I'm afraid that was the only attitude this working girl could cop, and I had no choice otherwise. See, there was safety and security in this arena of employment: drag offered me a legitimate way to earn a living not as an *impersonator*, like some

LET US ENTERTAIN YOU!

TINA DEVORE
Show Director

TIGER LIL
Choreographer

TERRY D.
Assistant Choreographer

LADY CHABLIS
Miss Chez Cabaret, 1977

CRYSTAL LAMBEGA
Miss Tri-State

RON ELLIS
Exciting & Electrifying

Cameo appearances by
TIASHA WALLIS

Lights By:
PATRICK

MICKEY DAY
Your Host & EmCee

The Onyx

SEPTEMBER 26TH & 27TH
OKLAHOMA
OCTOBER 4TH
MISS NEWCOMER OF THE YEAR
OCTOBER 17TH
ANNIVERSARY PARTY
EVERY THURSDAY
AUCTION NIGHT

341 West Peachtree - 523-9105

mighta called it, but as a woman. I wasn't some sorta "gender fugitive" in a gay bar, plus I really liked being a performer. So I guess I could deal with a li'l on-the-job racism.

One of the bartenders actually called me a "pickaninny," but he used that term ironic'ly to build my self-esteem. He wanted to

make me realize that I had a helluva lot more going for me than to be cast off as some dumb lackey with a good figure. He was always taking me shopping to make sure that I had something new to wear for the next show. He'd even take my pay and hold it till it was time to pay my bills. Mostly, he wanted to make sure I understood what grown-up responsibility was all about. That bartender's name was Bill Sullivan, and he taught me how to make my way. I'll always be grateful to him for that. But like many of the friends I've lost, he's now dead from AIDS.

I had a home and a job that first year or so in Atlanta. Y'might wonder what more a drag queen needed? Well, how 'bout estrogen! I got introduced to "hormones" from some of the prostitutes I knew, who had themselves some *fine-ass* titties. I was more than mildly curious 'bout how they *acquired* 'em, and when I found out, I demanded a set of my own. So they sent me to the big midtown hospital to call on a physician named Michael Feinberg.

I told Dr. Feinberg exactly what I wanted to do, and he sent me to a psychiatrist for 'bout a month, once or twice a week. That was part of the deal, to make sure I was some kinda serious. The headshrinker determined what I was and wanted to be, just as The Doll'd always known, only she didn't have herself the license to give Dr. Feinberg the go-ahead to start administering her estrogen prescriptions. I began with the ol'-fashioned Estradiol and Provera combo; both of which've been favorably replaced since then by Premarin. *Just in case y'not a pharmacist.*

The good doctor musta realized I was a woman in need of breast enhancement, too, but I coulda told him that without going through four weeks of psychiatry, which was almost as taxing as writing this book. After the second week of pill taking, Dr. Feinberg decided to increase my hormone treatment with breast shots, and not so long after, my titties were in bloom.

I also began noticing other changes in my body—y'know, like the veins in my arms went away, my voice got softer and higher. I was tweezing my eyebrows more, but there was really no need, 'cause the hair wasn't coming in as fast. My skin had got so soft, I'd kissed the Jergens good-bye. Plus, I'd wake up in the morning and find that I couldn't get a hard-on. Dead to the world. I loved that feature most!

I also began electrolysis, but stopped after I discovered it was too costly. I didn't have the convenience of being able to regularly afford up to a hundred dollars a week to have it done. Folks never realize that this process costs thousands and thousands of dollars just to do it right.

My name was now getting out to other clubs in Atlanta, where they'd started hearing 'bout "The Lady Chablis." I was getting noticed, building a reputation and even somewhat of my own following. But one night, though, in the midst of all my ascending glory, Jim Nally got pissed about something—who remembers what—and called me a *nigger* for the last time as far as I was concerned. This was after I'd kinda gotten up there with the audiences, bringing in more business to the bar. *His bar.* I wasn't seeing a penny more in my paycheck. So I up and quit the Onyx.

Without all of that money I'd grown accustomed to earning, I had to make some serious decisions 'bout what to do next. I thought 'bout my situation: I had these nice titties, but my name was still *legal'y* Benjamin. So I resigned myself to getting up early each morning, putting on the cutest li'l dress I owned, some conservative pumps, a min'mum amount of makeup, and off I went to pound the pavement as a professional woman, the classifieds tucked under my arm. I knew qualifying for a job'd be the easy part. The tough part was whether or not they'd question the name I'd chosen to put on the application: Brenda Dale Knox.

In retrospect, the only time anybody'd find out was when my Social Security number revealed my real name to my employers during tax time. Yeah, I lost a few jobs 'cause of that. But I mostly worked in positions long enough where I felt comfortable telling a manager or supervisor my T. I'd either confided in 'em, or they'd figured it out and didn't give a shit. Hell, I've only had my name legally changed from Benjamin Edward to Brenda Dale for the last five years.

Well, the first job I got was at a restaurant called the Prince George Inn, which just so happened to be a gay-owned joint. I worked there for 'bout a year as a salad person. This was when I got out of the show life for a while. I liked it better working a daily job, 'cause the perk was that I got to meet all these li'l *straight* boys. Yeah, girl, every restaurant's got a few of 'em on their waitstaff. A lotta the other employees at this restaurant knew about me, 'cause they'd seen me do my shows. But at the Prince George Inn, my being a full-time woman wasn't a problem.

Specially with this one waiter by the name of Mohammed Vartanian—him and I had this li'l love affair going at the restaurant. He was Middle Eastern of some sort and putting himself through school at Georgia Tech, where he was working on a lotta *B.S.* in chemical engineering. The Doll'd landed herself a tall, hairy scientist who studied a lot. I think she fell in love. No, girl, it was more like she'd *slipped*, 'cause I don't think true romance commences with the salad course, now, does it?

But once the folks at work found out that we was carrying on, the kids there started teasing the shit outta him, and he sorta turned away from me. I was hurt 'cause I really cared for this guy. And y'had to know I did if I tell y'that I spent most nights at his apartment watching him read. Oooh, I was gonna miss the way he licked his thumb and turned the pages, but I was also kinda glad that the door'd swung wide open to all the other men of Atlanta.

Just the same, I gotta give Mohammed his due. He *was* my first significant relationship there, and even my first *serious* relationship, period—not like Larry Marks or Sammy Green or any high-school-sweetheart kinda thing. No, no, baby. Mohammed represented the first time I said to myself, Oh, my God! I got husband material on my hands—let's head for the chapel! Yeah, I was caught up in all of that whirlwind fantasy with this Arabian stallion.

I quit working at the Prince George Inn in late 1975, 'cause I'd had my break from the show world and I wasn't planning on a life filled with lettuce and cucumbers. I'd moved to Atlanta to seek my peaches and dreams, not to sail the Seven Seas. But I didn't exactly have another drag job lined up neither, so I went to work for Eckerd's Drugstore, again as Brenda Knox.

Round this same time, I moved with Miss Tina Devore to a new house in DeKalb County. She took the upstairs quarters, along with some other drag kids, and I opted for the basement apartment. Well, it wasn't really an apartment, more like a room, a basement room that had a cobwebbed brick wall with the dirt seeping through from the cracks of cement. My new digs were a li'l spartan, but it was the first by-myself place I'd ever lived in. Most of all, this dirt den afforded me some privacy.

Miss Tina'd wanted me to live upstairs with her, but I insisted that I needed to be alone. It wasn't that I couldn't live with her. It's just that I was no longer a "drag queen," in the professional sense, like her and her roommates. I think I hurt Miss Tina by this altogether, 'cause I'd separated myself socially from that world, too. But this period of time was to be my hiatus from drag, and it would last for almost half a year.

Soon after I moved in, though, I got sick and was laid up for nearly a month in this dank basement, shivering and sneezing and wishing that God Himself woulda sent down an angel and carted me off to that big place in the heavens where all good ex-drag queens go. On toppa that, my sick leave didn't extend to three weeks of downtime, so I had to quit my job at Eckerd's. Soon my funds stopped coming in.

One day, my friend Linda came by to see me and was horrified that I was so sick and so cold. Well, no heating'll do it to y'every time. She packed up my stuff, put me in a housecoat that was a li'l short on style, and took me to her place on the other side of the city, out in the suburb of Smyrna, where she also lived alone. She worked for an insurance company during the day, and at night she was an usher at one of the coliseums, where they booked all the major acts that came to Atlanta.

Another move in less than a month. This time, I'm shacked up with Miss Linda in a new two-bedroom apartment. I got a white best girlfriend—a *real* girl—who started teaching me the ways of the white-woman's world. And with the last of my two-week paycheck from Eckerd's, I could open my first checking account. Now all's I needed was another job. Enter the Burlington Coat Factory Outlet and my new position as a salesclerk in women's coats.

In the meantime, Linda got herself a better job, as a stripper. She was working full-time and making close to a thousand dollars a night, getting tickets to fly anywhere and all these diamond rings from her thankful audiences. She even went out and bought herself a brand-new Chrysler Cordoba.

"We're moving!" she said.

Where to this time? A *real* uptown-white-woman's apartment

at a place called Regency Woods, in town. Gate, security, all of that. Encouraged by Linda's lush life and all our new trappings, I decided I needed to get back to the stage myself, so I quit Burlington and started my drag again—y'know, some li'l contests here and there.

"I'll pay your entry fee," said Linda every time, hoping I'd return perm'nently to performing. I'd enter a contest, then another, and another—small titles I needed to gather if I was gonna jump-start my abandoned career. Then I entered the Miss Dixieland Pageant. And won. The Doll was back. New and *improved*. After I won that crown, I got a job offer from the Locker Room, which was a show bar, a disco, a bathhouse, and a movie theater, all on different levels.

This was certainly a new experience for me. A bathhouse with nothing but naked men walking round? It was a job I looked forward to *handling*! As a cast member of the show, I was making like $175 a week more than I was at the Onyx. And all I did back in 1976 was lip-synch and dance. My monologues would come later.

Well, one particular night I was doing the show and afterward, this gay guy named Danny came up to me.

"Chablis, this friend that I used to go to school with is leaving next week to enlist in the army. He's a straight guy, and he's never been in a gay bar before, and he just saw your show and went absolutely crazy for you!"

On Friday night of the same week, Danny showed up again.

"Chablis, that guy I told you about is asking me to bring him back to say hello. He really wants to meet you."

"Well, where is this li'l child?" I inquired. "Lemme meet this li'l boy before he goes off to the army!"

And out from behind Danny he appeared. Five foot nine inches. Sandy brown hair. And a taut, muscular frame. A grin as wide as the Grand Canyon. And unless he'd worked at a deli, the cut of his inseam suggested he was damn glad to see me.

"Lady Chablis, I'd like for you to meet my friend Kenny Reardon."

Kenny came back that Saturday night, and we talked and stuff, and he kept saying that he couldn't believe I was really a guy.

"Y'better believe it, 'cause I really am. But it's not like I brag 'bout it, so keep it to y'self!" I joked. "Now, you, dear Kenny, are enrolled in the army, is it? So why are y'so concerned 'bout what *I* am?" I teased some more.

The next thing I knew he'd come over to Linda's for dinner one night while she was out. Child, I don't need to tell you that I put a cooking down! Complete with my famous southern cuisine. Well, Kenny never joined the armed services. And from that day on we were inseparable. A few months later, he gave me a ring that I continue to wear. A simple gold band I treasure to this day.

"Lady, I want you to marry me."

"Marry you?" There I went, feeling all *real* again. God, I must be good! I have worn that ring ever since the day he gave it to me. It was a spiritual gesture. No, we weren't calling the preacher or announcing it to the *Journal-Constitution*. In *our* hearts, we were already wed. And I became the closest thing he had to family, since he wasn't close to the one he'd left behind in Alabama.

On toppa that, we was both making good money—me at the Locker Room and him driving a truck for a liquor distributor. And since we had our material needs pretty much covered now, we could afford to be a li'l generous when another friend of mine decided to move to Atlanta from Tallahassee with his girlfriend. We were looking to start fresh, and they were having problems finding a place to get settled, so I left Linda to herself, and the four of us got ourselves a two-bedroom apartment. Me and Kenny and Randy and Duchess. She was a girl like me, and he was a white guy like Kenny, so we made a fine foursome.

After I'd won the Miss Gay World Pageant, I knew it was time to take my act on the road, play some of the other drag clubs in the big cities of the South. The new Lady Chablis had come back slowly but surely. And the Bicentennial Bitch was titled again. I began traveling to South Carolina and Alabama and to other places in Georgia, like Savannah. I had one gig to play at a joint called the Yum-Yum Tree in Montgomery, and since this was in Kenny's home state, he came along.

We pulled up in what I thought was a parking space right near the club's entrance. No sooner had I turned off the ignition when a police officer pulled up behind my li'l white Maverick. I poked my head outta the window and asked if I could park there.

"Ma'am, what's your name?" the officer asked all curious-like, without answering my parking question. I looked over at Kenny, who was just as puzzled.

"My name is Brenda Knox, *may I park here?*" I asked again, while Kenny sat looking straight ahead.

"May I see your driver's license, ma'am?" Kenny gave me a slight shrug and whispered in my ear to cooperate. Surely this was all some *hoogie's* way of tormenting a black girl.

"Ma'am, your driver's license says *Benjamin Knox.* What's goin' on here?"

Uh-oh.

"Well, Brenda Knox is the name that I go by," I returned confidently.

"What are you talkin' about, that's the name you go by. *What is your name?*'

"My name *is* Benjamin Knox, but I *use* Brenda Knox."

"Ma'am, excuse me, but something ain't right here. Would you please step out of the car?"

Instant terror. Child, I hadn't got so much as my left pump outside that Ford when the officer pulled out a set of handcuffs and arrested me for—get this one—"falsification of identification."

And then he took my purse outta my hand and poured everything out on the hood of the car. Great. Maybelline eyeliner, three stamps, my wallet, and a joint. I'm standing there with my hands cuffed behind my silken back, tears streaming down my face. I musta been some sight with that Miss Gay World crown on my head.

"That's mine," Kenny pleaded to the officer, who was inspecting the drugs from my purse. "Please don't take her. Take me," Kenny begged, but the cop wasn't budging. This was Alabama: there's no good reason to take a white boy to jail if y'can find a black one instead, specially if the nigger's queer and wearing a dress. So they took her purse and her gowns, and they whisked The Doll off to jail. Alabama! Home of redneck, nigger-hating sons of bitches! And y'can bet they had a heyday with me.

When Kenny and Nick Scout, the owner of the Yum-Yum Tree, finally came and got me, six or seven hours later, Kenny held me all night and we just cried and cried. "Baby, we'll get through this.

Whatever it takes," he tried to assure me. "If I have to rob a bank, whatever it takes, we'll take care of this. Don't you worry. We'll get you a good lawyer," he promised.

But Nick Scout had to put up his club and its property to get me out. The bail was twenty thousand dollars. Big. And that's when I knew I was in trouble. The next day Nick took me to his lawyer. Her name was Melissa DeLane, and to this day, I've promised myself, when I get all my money from this damn book y'reading, I'm gonna find that woman and pay her.

And, oh, was she a powerful black woman. Miss Melissa DeLane had it going on, child. My first thought when she extended her hand to greet me was, this bitch ain't gonna take no shit from white folks, that's for damn sure!

She told me right flat out: "You're looking at six to twelve years, and they will go after you. You're gay, you're black, you dress as a woman, and you're in Alabama." Girlfriend was some kinda direct, now, wasn't she?

"...But we have one thing going for us if you can prove it...that you've lived as Brenda Dale Knox."

Hell, *yeah*!

"I got letters from my gran'mama that's addressed Brenda Dale Knox. I got a light bill with Brenda Dale Knox on it. My estrogen prescription says Brenda Dale Knox on the label," I said, knowing that this was a matter of survival. She nodded slowly and offered a short smile.

The night before court she called me.

"Brenda, I want you to show up tomorrow for court like you would if you were going to church," she directed. And I said okay.

So I filed into court the next day, honey, with Kenny on one arm and Nick Scout on the other. Then once the proceedings began, Miss Melissa DeLane stood up, tall and regal.

"Your Honor, these officers had no probable cause to arrest my client even if she did have drugs on her. They had no probable cause to want to search her purse for anything. And I am here to prove that there was no falsification of identification."

And she began proving stuff, baby—that I was Brenda Dale Knox.

"Look at her, Your Honor: How would she look telling someone that her name was Benjamin Knox? This is how she has to live every day. She is used to offering Brenda Dale Knox as her full name when asked. Look at her. Look at these forms. Here is a letter from her grandmother."

And then the judge questioned the police officers. They got up and did their thing, but it was all inconsequential. And the judge concluded, "Due to lack of evidence, this case is dismissed."

Yes, child, the Lord was on my side again in Montgomery, Alabama. That legal-eagle black bitch got The Doll off! The case was dismissed. And after all of that happened, I was still Miss Gay World.

ANATOMIC'LY

CORRECT

CHAPTER 6

WAS MY CAREER as a woman worth a few scares with the law? That Alabama incident really got me thinking 'bout whether I should continue a public life in drag as The Lady Chablis or go back to living as Brenda—Miss Tupperware with a nine-to-five existence. I also had to decide if I wanted to be a real woman, *in the surgical sense,* or if I wanted to be a female impersonator, privately as well as profession'ly. I became very reclusive. I didn't go anywhere. It was like a nervous breakdown and a delayed reaction, of sorts, to the trauma of Alabama. I started worrying 'bout losing Kenny, too, though he'd constantly reassure me that everything was fine. But I knew it wasn't.

Kenny told me to take as much time as I needed to get my thoughts together, but he was mostly on the road, dealing with what happened to me all by himself. Thank God, then, for the kindness of Randy and Duchess. They did their best to hold me up, while I recoiled from all of that mess in Montgomery. They've been together for like fifteen years now. She's black, transsexual, and looks just like me. He's my age and white, 'bout six foot three. As a matter of fact, he's even from my hometown. We'd often sit round and reminisce about the town neither one of us could flee fast enough from.

Duchess was from Marianna, Florida, which is like forty miles outside of Quincy, but they met at a gay bar in Tallahassee. Denise—Duchess was her stage name—tried a career as a show-girl, but it wasn't for her. So she decided she'd become a real woman and live that way—y'know, have the operation and all. And she did. When I first met her, I'd only been in Atlanta a year or so, and she and Randy were just two guys in love. Yeah, Randy's a big ol' sissy, too. But at that time, I was going through my own transition, growing titties to complement my appearance as a girl. So Duchess, who's exactly my size, musta seen me as a role model, 'cept she was determined to take it a step farther and become a transie.

"Once y'make the decision, there's really no turnin' back," I said.

"I know."

"Y'have to be sure this is what y'wanna do, 'cause, honey, we're talkin' a twenty-four-hour-a-day job."

"I know."

"It's not as simple as y'think it is."

"I know."

"Y'gotta make sure that y'family's ready for it."

"I know."

"And that y'got the wardrobe waitin' when y'titties start to grow."

Who the hell was I to be giving this poor thing the third degree? I musta realized then that a large portion of my own depression centered on the indecision over who and what I was. It wasn't enough to call myself a "woman," when I couldn't physically prove it to anybody who might call it into question. Though y'mama's real good at camouflaging the facts, that incident in Alabama was a wake-up call to reality, and if it happened once so arbitrar'ly, it could prob'ly happen over and over again in my lifetime. 'Less I wanted to be seen as a freak forever, I needed to go one way or the other, and right quick, before I wound up dead.

I began questioning myself, 'cause I wasn't sure if one day I might wanna go back and be Benjamin. I knew I was very fem'-nine and beautiful, but I'd started meeting masculine gay men, too. There was no proof that all gay men had to be sissies; most, in fact, are not. But I was from a place where y'gender and behavior were s'pposed to be one and the same. Black *or* white, real cut and dry. If they weren't, y'were prob'ly s'pposed to be the other—so y'somehow became it. 'Cause where I came from, there wasn't any such thing as *in-between*.

Maybe I had a chance, after all, to be a fine, gay man myself. Wouldn't I find more security as a gay *guy* than feeling inadequate as *half* a woman, always fearful that a straight man might someday leave me for a fish? All these things were passing through my thoughts when I decided that I just didn't want to be no man, no matter what the consequences were.

But I *was* beginning to feel as if I wasn't real, just the same; that I wasn't sincere somehow—like I was fooling everybody. I'd taken good care of the outside, visible part of me without giving any attention to what I wanted on the inside. I was still not really happy with who or what I'd become. No, I didn't wanna be no man, but I wasn't certain that I had much choice when it came down to definition. (Something was very much missing: maybe it was the determination to believe in my instincts.) But I also wondered, Why not a sex-change? I mean, I just couldn't be going round with titties and a dick all my life. I'd have to make some kinda decision.

I asked myself, Which was more important, that I live my life the way that I think it ought to be lived, or that I live my life according to the way society wants me to? It seemed clear to me that it was more important that I live my life according to the way I wanted to, but I'd also have to do it in a way that nobody could question and do it so well that anybody who didn't agree with my decision at least had to respect me for it.

"Growin' up, we knew y'was a bit of a sissy, but *now* y'given us something *else* to deal with," was my aunt Ella Mae's first response to the sight of her nephew wearing a handkerchief dress and a pair of sling-backs. "What about the preacher who *baptized* you?"

"What about him?" I asked.

"What about all the folks who supported you in church 'cause they thought *you'd* end up bein' a minister?" she pressed.

"Let 'em crown me an African *priestess* for all I give a shit, Aunt Mae."

"But, baby, are y'*happy*?" Gran'mama interrupted, concerned only 'bout my well-being.

"I'm some kinda happy, Gran'mama. I think I know who I am now."

It took my moving away to Atlanta and coming home for my daddy's funeral before I walked into my gran'mama's house wearing a dress. I'd never worn a dress in her presence while I lived in Quincy or Tallahassee. Hell, I'd never even smoked in front of her.

Now I do both. But once Gran'mama saw me in a dress and everything was cool, that was the *only* acceptance I needed. Aunt Ella Mae, y'can pout all you want and call it a sin, 'cause my gran'mama has given me the *okay,* which means the resta y'all can *kiss my ass!* Everybody pretty much fell in line after Gran'mama.

But then a li'l religion entered into it, too. After I felt comfortable with myself, and I got the approval from the folks at home, and I didn't give a damn about society anymore, the only real seal of approval I needed was from the Lord Himself.

I began praying. Hard. I asked God to tell me if I was doing the right thing, to gimme a signal and lemme know. I told the Lord that I was gonna continue to do this, and if it wasn't right, to please put an obstacle in my path and turn me round right quick. I kept praying on it, and one day, all of the sex-change issues came into some kinda focus: I really didn't want an operation, didn't need one. It wasn't the answer. I was just as legitimate as a woman who'd kept her candy, if I believed with all my heart and soul that I was one. An operation could only allow my full-length mirror to tell me what I already knew and felt inside, but it wasn't gonna make those feelings and that knowledge any stronger. Just more anatomic'ly correct.

But I couldn't be the same Lady Chablis without my candy. I couldn't be the same Brenda Dale Knox without it. Or the same Edward, who my family loved. Or the same Miss Pee-Wee, who Connie and Miss Rhonda Conyers once knew. No, I'd be somebody totally different. So, how could I make surgical alterations to myself and still be true to the folks who loved me, when I worked so hard to become who I was with the full support of their good graces? Y'take away my candy and I'd be just another fish. But never again the unique lady that I'd made myself into.

I was liberated. So, question it if y'wanted to, but that's who I was and who I was always gonna be. I began realizing that I had myself a personality, too. *Stop playing them roles y'think people wanna see, Chablis, and just be y'self.* Boom! A new door is opened for me: my humor emerged when I proudly revealed myself to the world. If I could touch people's lives with my humor and make 'em laugh with my honesty, then this self-discovery thing had a lot going for it.

Finally I was ready to go back to the gay scene, not onstage necessarily, but just out in the clubs, watching the shows, walking through the audiences, and stirring up a li'l curiosity.

"That's Lady Chablis!" I'd hear 'em whisper. "Where's she been?"

She'd been easing back into it, honey—that's where. And she still had that air about her that she ain't no drag queen! No, child, The Doll was a *real* woman, so don't be associating her with the stage life! Don't misread me, I've done well by a career on stage, but I just wasn't gonna let my identity and my profession share the same answer to the same question.

Shortly after I found myself, I went out on the town, all bubbling over with my fem'nine mystique, to a new nightclub called Illusions, with my friends John and Thomas, a professional black couple who've since then become as close to me as family. Kenny was with us, too. And we were sitting there watching a show, and next to us was this table of guys. We started conversatin' with 'em, and all of us agreed to meet there again the following weekend. One of the folks at that table was a guy named Shawn, who'd just graduated from Georgia State. Sandy brown hair and a beautiful six-foot-tall swimmer's physique, him and I just clicked. After that, we'd chat on the phone any chance we got, and he'd even drive me to my outta-town bookings, which were the only drag engagements I was accepting right 'bout now, since Kenny was mostly on the road himself and I felt like some kinda third-wheel widow with Randy and Duchess. Shawn kept me company through it all, and I began referring to him as my drag son.

Well, doesn't my drag son get a job as a male stripper? This other guy named Max, who also sat at that Illusions table the night we'd all met, decided to put together an all-male, traveling strip show. And since Max had been a radio personality, it was his job to emcee. Shawn got Max to add me to the revue, so they asked me to go with 'em for this opening-night gig in Athens, Georgia, to fill in between the guys' numbers with a li'l show of my own. Our new name: The Men in Motion featuring The Lady Chablis.

Max got sick at the last minute and wasn't gonna make it. But without Max, we had no emcee. We thought of canceling, but couldn't, 'cause we'd signed a contract to be the lead act of this new club's first night. I spoke up right away and brazenly said that I could do what Max did, *easily.* Honey, I'd been waiting for the day when it'd be my turn at the mike, and now my number had come up.

No question, girl—The Doll had 'em tipping! And since Max wasn't gonna argue with that kinda success, the next show got renamed: The Lady Chablis and *Her* Men in Motion.

The following weekend a new club was opening in Atlanta, and we got booked to do the same number. All the kids from the other clubs came out, and this marked the first time they got to see me with a microphone and a monologue. After that appearance, my phone was ringing off the hook.

So during the time I was spreading my gospel in Atlanta, I'd come down to Savannah with my Men in Motion to do a show at the Friends Lounge, one of two gay clubs in Savannah, and strictly cabaret. I don't need to tell y'now that the crowd loved The Doll. 'Cause the next thing I knew, Bobby Ray Benson, the owner, invited me back for an encore the following weekend— *by myself.* So I broke it to the Men in Motion that I was gonna try my hand at flying solo, now that the rebirthed Lady Chablis— the girl who sang and danced—*could also do stand-up.*

Whenever I performed my monologue, I made sure to comb the audience for a "victim." I'm always gonna pick on someone— that's part of my act. Still is. I'll usually find somebody in the front row who's got a certain *afraid* look on their face, like "Oh my God, please don't say nothing to me." *That's when I move in for the kill.* If I see a woman, and she's draped in diamonds, I might ask, "Girl, what didja do to get those jewels? Didja suck dick that good? Share y'secrets with The Doll!"

I look for li'l things in people to poke fun at. But if I find a person who ain't handling it well, I'll make sure that I've brought the joke back round so that the laugh is ultimately on me. I don't put myself on a pedestal. And I let folks know that when they've tipped me, they've just paid my light bill or something. That way they know how much I appreciate their patronage.

That night's victim spotted: an elderly white gentleman— very uptown-looking in his seersucker suit and white patent leather loafers—sitting with his companion, equal parts frail and effem'nate.

"You, sir, in the front row…Yeah, *you*, child…Why y'looking at me funny like that, fella?" No response from either of 'em. Fear and shrugging was all Miss Seersucker's pacemaker was gonna muster, I decided, by the petrified stare he returned. "Is my Kotex hanging out? Or did my clit *wave* at you or something?" I interrogated him, as he shook his head back 'n' forth right quick as if I was looking for the correct answer. *No, just a tip!*

"What is it, baby?" I continued, stroking his face while I parked it in his lap, facing him. The beads of sweat was gathering on his forehead like they'd been called to a family reunion. I brushed his brow several times with the same warm hand that held my microphone, then I'd wipe it playfully across his chest. My touch musta turned him into a cadaver, 'cause he was froze solid. "Yoo-hoo…What's wrong, child…y'don't like chocolate? Or y'don't like chocolate with *nuts*?" I thought Gran'pa was gonna buy the farm right then and there—not that I noticed him opening his checkbook none!

Unfazed, I returned to the lower platform of the stage to take a bow and collect my applause.

"Thank y'all, and remember now, if y'driving home, don't be doing it drunk. My tips is *not* y'bail money!"

That initial visit led to a regular booking and the start of my fan club in Savannah. I took on a few gigs with the Motion Men, and set out with Shawn for three nonstop months on the road, back-and-forth, and fully booked. The only glitch was that Kenny and I never saw one another: On the days he was off, I was gone. And vice-versa. I missed our marriage, but I felt my time had come. I'd reconciled my demons, knew what I wanted outta my career, and sought to achieve it all.

I was gone for a few weeks when I shot home to pick up some things before leaving again. Kenny wasn't there, and he was s'pposed to be, but he never came home the entire weekend. Left no note. And he always left me a note, notes everywhere. But nothing this time.

Well, I canceled everything, 'cause I wasn't moving till my husband came home and I knew he was all right. So I waited: Friday, Saturday, and Sunday, then Monday—still no Kenny. On Tuesday, he finally showed up, and he had this look on his face that I'd never seen.

"I rode with somebody else in their truck and made a delivery in Florida," he said sheepishly. And I kinda let it slide. Then he stroked my face. I smiled, and before long, we kissed. We made love. After we finished I asked him again.

"Are y'gonna tell me the truth now? What's going on?"

He sighed.

"Well, I've been with this lady, a Mexican lady. I've been with her all weekend," he said, apologetically. Maybe even a li'l remorsefully, but it was too late.

"Kenny, it's over. I can't deal with the fact that y'bold-faced lied and then fucked me. Here y'had me thinking you was dead somewhere." I was crushed. But there wasn't a doubt in my mind that I could never love him again.

"Lady, I've invested all this time into you...." He tried negotiating.

"Kenny, y'ain't invested *shit* into me. But I wanna know, What'd y'all do?" I demanded. He looked at me petrified. "*I wanna know!*" He didn't say a word. "Was it her *pussy* y'liked so much?" Girl, I was enraged.

I leaned over and picked up the iron that stood on the nightstand closer to his side of our bed and busted him one upside the head before he could even realize I'd done it. My baby sat there stunned, as a bloody faucet started streaming down his naked shoulders and backside. He picked up a dirty towel from the laundry pile on the floor nearby and began wiping the blood off. I just looked at him with disgust. He moaned in pain for like a minute as he held his head from bleeding with the same shirt he'd worn when he'd got home. Now I looked away, hurt beyond all hell, while he got up slowly, threw on his pants, and ran outta our bedroom door for the very last time.

TWO TEARS

IN A

BUCKET

CHAPTER 7

WHATEVER...

NOW I WAS back on my own again. Divorced. Kept his ring. Still wear it even.

Kenny moved out, but the aroma of his musk lingered in our bedroom till it all kinda weakened and vanished a few weeks later—a replay of his presence and his absence. I'd arranged for Randy and Duchess to deliver the bag I'd packed for him to the Mexican lady's place, where he was now taking up full residence and, in less than a year, would marry and give her a daughter. I was left with my roommates, both working my last nerve with all their pampering, and both of them a visible reminder of what a happy *heterosexual* marriage looked like.

I knew I needed to get back into the swing of the gay world, 'cause that'd been the only constant in my life. The show stage was where I belonged, where I never fucked up, where I'd known very few losses. Titles and applause were the payoff, I guess, for a life spent denying what I was—not to mention the tips and steady pay.

But emotionally, I was lost. The gravity of what I'd done to Kenny had just sunk in, and I felt suicidal for almost a month. I left Randy and Duchess to hide out at my friend Earl's place, where I could collect my thoughts in peace and not have to be reminded of my recent divorce every time I looked at my room-mates. A fan since my days at the Onyx, Earl was a computer technician who worked the graveyard shift, and when he was home, he was usually sleeping. The upshot was that I plunged myself into my work, taking as many outside bookings as I could. My stage work and my isolation kept me sane for the first month.

I couldn't hide out at Earl's forever, but I knew I needed to let Randy and Duchess get on with their lives, so I talked my friend Shawn into becoming my roommate at an apartment complex called the Briarwood. We just applied one day, went back the next, put our money down, got the keys, and moved in. At least something in my life, besides my work, was going off without a hitch.

Shawn and me'd just got ourselves settled when our doorbell rang for the first time. "Y'all get high, *hon?*" said our new neighbor, Miss Denise. Oooh, I knew Miss Denise and me were gonna be *real* good friends. She lived by herself with a li'l poodle named Jocco. Miss Denise'd have me over for dinner a couple times a week, and we'd be in and outta each other's apartments like we was Lucy and Ethel. She liked Shawn, too, but she never got past believing he was my boyfriend. Never dawned on her once that he was gay, 'cause she didn't even guess what I was. Girlfriend didn't have a clue, and I was starting to feel a li'l dishonest.

"Miss Denise, I got somethin' to tell you."

"What is it, *hon?*"

"I think I need to tell y'this, 'cause it would make me feel more *free* round you." I wasn't sure how I was gonna say it, 'cause the blank look on her face was waiting for anything.

"Well, tell me, *hon*," she said, eagerly inviting my response as her long gold nails danced across my kneecap, her anticipation punctured by nothing 'cept optimism.

"I'm gonna tell y'flat out, 'cause there's no other way to say it: I'm a sex-change. I used to be a guy till I had the operation."

She was the one and only person I ever told this lie to.

"Oh. That's nice, *hon*." Big smile. But no reaction, like I'd handed her the weekly circular from the Food Lion.

And to this day, Miss Denise still thinks I'm a transie! I've never told her the truth 'cause I've let it go so long. I'd be afraid she'd think I was some kinda liar. See, hiding my candy wasn't just a way to negotiate the bedroom with a man. It sometimes became a way of life that infiltrated all avenues of my personal relations. By this point in my adulthood, I could count on one hand the number of folks I'd been able to completely open up to without holding anything back. Believe me, my steps toward true liberation were always dictated by the tolerance of others. Isn't it usually s'pposed to be the other way around?

Shawn possessed that youthful masculinity, the kind that's reckless and cute all at once. My Man in Motion found gay life still new to him, so that handsome motherfucker treated me like

I was his wife and mentor. He was always protectively putting his arm round me and pecking me on the cheek in public. Clearly, our friendship was as novel to him as it was to me.

Even our friends thought we were lovers. He'd come to every show, bring in my gowns, and have my shooter of apple schnapps ready for me at the bar after I stepped offstage. I think in a way he had a crush on me, and I know I had a crush on him, but we both knew it was just a harmless li'l thing. It was hard *not* to fall in love with somebody who treated me as considerately as he did, and, above all, he was the one who gave me my first real Christmas, which still stands out as one of the most significant gifts I've ever received.

It was like five in the morning when I returned to discover the splendor of the holiday that most folks take for granted. I'd gone outta town for a booking that he couldn't go with me to, but my darling roommate went out and bought us a tree—the big flocked kind, 'cause y'gotta simulate that look of snow when y'live in the South. We didn't have a whole lotta money, but he managed to find some real pretty ornaments: what appeared to be a hundred multicolored balls with gold glitter, and lotsa tiny lights, which our long-branched Scotch pine took to wearing like a drag queen does rhinestones and bugle beads. I was so *impressed*. Under the tree, and resting on a red-felt skirt, were all these gifts, each one with a different wrapping, and every single one of 'em said my name on the card.

I just sat there in awe, staring, and indulging in what I'd always thought was a fantasy made just for television. I looked down at the bib of my taffeta dress to see the polka dots left from all my boohooin'. I couldn't recall when a single gesture meant so much. My long, loud sob musta stirred him from his slumber.

"Merry Christmas, Brenda," he said, almost sleepwalking when he leaned down to plant a big quiet kiss on my forehead.

"Yes, child, Merry Christmas."

SHAWN AND ME were some kinda happy together, and I was dwelling less on Kenny, but, during the course of my show life, I found me another lover that turned out to be more abusive than any man I knew. I got introduced to Miss Crystal Meth herself, which was like a marriage of speed and cocaine, so y'might imagine the buzz she offered up as a courting ritual. Oooh, I loved her, child. Thought I'd become The Bionic Doll as a result, 'cause I could go four or five days, never sleep, and get twice as much done as the average person.

Since I had lotsa time on my hands, I increased the amount of partying and shopping that typically filled my life, and even though I was doing my bookings and taking the occasional escort job, I still found myself short of cash every month. Miss Crystal Meth ain't cheap, and she was a habit I got increasin'ly dependent on to get me through the day, fooling me into believing I was more productive. I needed the exhilaration I felt on this drug 'cause she helped me medicate the traumas of my man troubles. And if I wasn't gonna be *do*mestic any longer, I'd have lotsa time to fill. That's when I decided to go into business for myself.

My whole life had been spent picking up after other people, whether it was Mama, my brothers, Connie, or my many husbands. So I thought, who better than The Doll to start up a cleaning service? But I didn't want folks confusing my day job with my evening activities, so I decided against using Chablis in the name—besides, *Dust Bunnies* had a better ring to it.

Business really caught on, but Miss Crystal Meth couldn't duplicate my efforts simultaneously, so it was time to take on an employee. Miss Denise found me a li'l black girl who lived in our complex and needed a job, since she wasn't going to school like most kids at fifteen. Tracey turned out to be a decent worker. She'd take a house and I'd take a house, and we'd get two places done in the same amount of time. For this, Tracey got four bucks an hour, under the table. So my li'l business grew some more, to where I again hired two other girls to come work for me. I did it all without paying taxes, too. That helped.

Seven-hundred dollars a week was my total income from all directions, but as fast as I made it, it'd fly out the door again: more dresses, more drugs. The Doll needed a raise in her salary. After all, she wasn't sleeping or eating much, and you'd be shocked to know how many hours of the day are given over to that. So why not add "drug dealer" to her résumé?

Looking back on it all, I can see it prob'ly wasn't even a question of extra income that led me to dealing. My own dealer would sell it to me for a certain amount, and it was up to me to recover my profit from that. But I was more interested in satisfying my habit, so being a dealer myself meant the added bonus of not having to pay top dollar for mine no more—and I could take as much as I needed right outta the stash.

But my moods were changing with my looks, and not for the better. The closer I was to my drugs, the better my mood, which bordered on evil till I could bring myself back up with another gram. My face was thinner, and it'd turned dirty brown from the cocoa glow that had once been part of my trademark complexion. No amount of makeup was gonna disguise this kinda decay or the huge pimples broken out on my face. My eyes, always doelike, were carrying heavier bags than I do to an outta-town booking. My lips even had a dry, colorless texture to 'em with distinct white stains of saliva—licking 'em as often as I did from being all jittered out on that shit. This was definitely a low point in The Doll's beauty history.

I was totally addicted. My enthusiam for performing was nothing compared to the speeding high and imagined energy I took from Miss Crystal herself. She became my world. I'd hit the booking circuit only if there was some real money to be made. Otherwise, I stuck close to home with my full-blown habit and Dust Bunnies to keep me occupied. As far as dealing in the club where I had a drag reputation and all, I never worried 'bout being watched by the undercover police. Too many other people were in the business of selling for just me to be singled out. I knew the only way I'd get caught was if I'd fucked somebody up with a bad batch. But no problem there, 'cause I sampled anything I sold. And I also knew that the folks I was selling it to didn't want no trouble, any more than I did. See, the bonds of confidentiality between a dealer and her client are the same as a lawyer's, child.

'Course what Shawn never counted on was his best friend and roommate stealing his money and not replacing it the way she used to when she was a li'l short and needed an overnight loan. And now she'd also become a full-fledged thief, taking what she could, whenever she could, to support a habit that meant more to her than her friends, and more to her than herself.

I came home one day with Li'l Leo, a bartender and a sometime lover of mine when either of us needed the human touch in between our respective relationships. Li'l Leo also was a big part of my dealing phase, 'cause he served as my distributor, of sorts. Like, he'd keep the drugs on him while I was doing my sales pitch, then I'd send the folks over to him for delivery. He even made house calls.

Anyway, we crept upstairs to Shawn's room one day to steal some cash, and instead we found a lock on the door. I was seething at the sight of this. But my Shawn'd finally caught on to y'mama's wicked ways and put a halt to the proceedings. Nevertheless, my anger got the best of me, and I told Li'l Leo to take a hike, while I hightailed it over to Shawn's job at the Peasant Restaurant—where I'd once done my baking stint.

"*Fuck* you, man, y'put a lock on your got-damn door," I began as I walked right up to him while he was marrying some ketchup bottles and filling salt 'n' pepper shakers.

"Brenda, I'm sick of my shit being missing. And I've noticed lately that somebody's been helping herself to my tips," he said without skipping a beat. "Do you understand that I don't trust you anymore? Or any of the people you bring in the house?" He was spitting as he spoke, he was so incensed. "The only way I knew how to stop you was to throw a lock on the door! At least till I can find someplace else to live!"

"What y'talkin' 'bout? You ain't movin'!"

"Oh, I'm moving all right. You're *not* the Brenda I used to know. You're somebody else, somebody sick and strung out. I just don't trust you," he said, fighting back tears and checking round to see if the manager wasn't in the vicinity.

"Y'put a lock on your door? You, my best friend and confidant, the person who's come to know more 'bout me than anybody else, the person who gave me my first flawless Christmas, the person who worshipped me? Have I disappointed and hurt y'this much that y'had to lock me outta y'room?"

I broke down, and Shawn put his arm round me and petted my cheek with the back of his hand. He told the Peasant staff that he had a family emergency and took the rest of the day off, then we took a long drive and tried to figure out what was next.

"Maybe you should get away for a while, Brenda," Shawn suggested. "Start over someplace where the living is easier and the temptations aren't so great."

I did know one friend I could depend on now to help remove me from the tawdry elements of Atlanta's gay club life. His name was Bill McDougal, and while I'd met him in the early years of my move to Atlanta, he'd since returned to quieter parts of Georgia, a small town outside of Albany. I'd first made his acquaintance through Miss Tina Devore. Then we became very close friends on our own, and a year or two after our friendship we sorta fell in love. Well, he fell in love with me, really. When I called him this time at his home in Leesburg, I told him I was gonna lose my mind and all my friends if I didn't get the hell outta town.

"I'll be there tomorrow," he guaranteed me.

So I left Dust Bunnies in Tracey's capable hands and said good-bye to Atlanta with an all-nighter, at Miss Denise's kind insistence. But I was still hungover in bed the next day when Bill's Ford van pulled up at Briarwood and took me to the li'l town that's just outside of Albany by twelve miles. I was headed back to Quincy in my mind, 'cause all small towns look like my hometown.

We pulled up in the night as we approached the front entrance to his mobile home, and I stepped outta the van very slowly. My ass was hurt from sitting so long, but I was also amazed at how surreal it all seemed in this dark envelope of an environment, where only blackness existed to color this landscape. *My new home,* I kept reminding myself. But anything this black seemed scary, child. Were all of them crickets singing a welcome chorus to The Doll? I wondered. Na-a-ah, musta been that she was still coming down from that hangover.

So we went in, and I met Bill's roommate, Jonathan Weber. He was a pianist, and Bill was an organist who also built and repaired them big pipe organs that y'find only in churches. Their trailer was a deluxe model and a far cry from Aunt Kate's own double-wide that I'd left back in Tallahassee. This one was full of plants and lotsa scriptures on the wall, pictures of Jesus everywhere, and lotsa homemade ashtrays and knicknacks. The built-in furnishings seemed new and christened with the dueling scents from their vast aftershave collection, which took up most of the space in the bathroom. The scents hung thick in the air that extended past a galley kitchen and into the three bedrooms.

I caused some friction with Bill and Jonathan from the minute I stepped inside. Theirs was a relationship on the wane, girl, so I didn't have to do too much to be the recipient of Jonathan's resentment. He knew all 'bout me, and for the year or two that Bill and him had been together, he knew damn well that Bill'd never gotten over me. But Bill's Christian values were at the heart of his allowing Jonathan to remain. This was one of the reasons I loved Bill so much, but it was also why things never worked out for him and me long-term.

Bill had begun going to church on a regular basis, to an open community place of worship that suited all denominations. Unitarian, I believe it was. From my first Sunday there it was apparent, by the reception I got when I walked in at his side, that he'd already told folks about his friend who was coming from Atlanta to move in, 'cause the other parishioners showered me with "Welcome, Brendas" and hugs galore. I mighta thought it was some kinda cult, the way they was behaving—all those touchy-feely, lemme-hug-you-and-love-you sorts of attitudes—but my urban cynicism was getting the best of me. I hadn't yet given this church a chance. These folks wanted nothing from me but the return of my self-fulfillment in the eyes of God.

Being back in a small town was like being thrown in the drunk tank. All I had to do was sit on my ass and recuperate, take my hormones—which I'd stopped during my binge with Miss Crystal Meth—and gain weight. I'd been down to 90 pounds, from the solid 115 I'd maintained all my adult life, but my weight would come back up now to a healthier 110, and my beauty would return herself from her hibernation just as fast.

After three weeks, I got a phone call from Li'l Leo. He'd packed up his car and come to Albany, where he had some family I never knew 'bout. He'd made connections with them to move down here just to be near me. Some nights he'd come and stay with me, which at first caused a li'l problem between him and

Bill, since that meant Leo would sleep in my bed, and Bill would have to sleep in his own. Bill liked having somebody next to him at night.

Bill also didn't think he liked or trusted Leo, so a li'l tug-o'-war over The Doll emerged, and she had to sit 'em both down while the law got laid out. She'd come here to regain her peace of mind. Every other concern was secondary. Is The Doll somewhat self-centered? Completely, but at least she admits it. Bill was initially ruffled by the fact that Leo'd packed up his stuff to come be with me, because Bill saw this time as an opportunity to give ourselves a chance again. Till Leo showed up, I didn't do anything to make him think otherwise.

Then, as if our lives weren't complicated enough, Bill's wife from an early marriage announced she was headed up from Florida with their two kids in tow. Now, Jonathan Weber sure wasn't gonna stay round for this revival of *The Brady Bunch,* so he took himself and his piano playing to that same restaurant in Atlanta where I'd once worked, The Prince George Inn.

Lorna, the ex-wife, was a country girl, uneducated but sincere from her heart. No pageant winner, she limped as a result of one leg being shorter than the other. What she didn't have in the looks department, she made up with her kindness and personality. It was evident from the start that Lorna loved her children and she loved her husband and she loved me. I'd come home from some of the bookings I'd now taken to support myself again, and she'd've washed my clothes and had 'em all laid across my bed. Had my dinner ready. Or lunch. Or breakfast. Didn't matter—she catered to my every need. She proved that she wasn't threatened by me. She was only there for the sake of her children and to help Bill and me with whatever she could offer—cleaning, cooking, running our errands. Lorna wasn't interested in coming between us, 'cause she knew the score. She just needed her children to be with their father, and I understood this entirely.

"I'm a father, Brenda, I have a responsibility to them," he said, as if apologizing for what that meant for us.

"Bill, y'forgettin' the fact that *I* never asked to be y'wife."

I loved those children. But kids were never in my plans, though his were abs'lutely wonderful. They were then ten and twelve, a girl and a boy, and they called me Auntie Brenda from the minute they walked in the door. Yeah, they knew that their father was gay. They knew 'bout me. We sat down and explained it all to 'em, as best as they could absorb it: why Bill slept in my bed and not with their mother, all that kinda stuff.

Bill allowed me to forget about those years in Atlanta, even a year or so later, when it was time for me to leave Leesburg. I was doing nothing there. The kids were there, the wife was there, Bill was happy, the children were happy, she was happy. But I was starting to grow restless. I'd got my health back and I was traveling again. I knew I needed something more than living in another double-wide trailer, even in a pretty place like Leesburg. The McDougals were now the family they always shoulda been, so it was time for me to move on.

Li'l Leo had himself a car, so I was gone like every other weekend at least, traveling back and forth mostly to work at the Friends Lounge, which was having financial troubles and needed a showcase boost. In fact, *Miss* Bobby Ray Benson, the owner, was 'bout to close it before she began booking me exclusively. Every time I performed, the place'd be packed with folks. Wall-to-wall, just to see The Doll. When Bobby Ray recognized that her bar might have a second wind, she offered me full-time employment, that is, if I'd consider moving my ass to Savannah. She guaranteed she'd pay to move me there and lemme work for the rent, utilities, and my portion of the phone bill.

For the first time in my career, I'd finally get to be the headliner. The club's stage would be mine, and I'd get to pick the other showgirls.

"Bobby Ray, I'm on my way!"

CORONA-

TION

STREET

CHAPTER 8

WONDER WOMAN (PERFORMING AT CLUB ONE, SAVANNAH)

Oooh, glorious Savannah!

From the second I got there I felt like a gay man's movie star, baby. There was no question 'bout it: my celebrity was *visible*. I could walk through all of them famous squares Savannah has and be recognized and fawned over. I was an *attraction*. And I loved every minute of it.

In a city the size of Savannah, the getting-to-know-y' kinds of opportunities meet y'head-on, no matter where y'go, so I was gonna take full advantage of this town's most accessible feature. Hell, it turned out to be good for business, too. Whatever I said, went—and the crowd was loving it. I was emceeing like never before, trying on new monologues as often as I change my tampons. I gotta thank Miss Bobby Ray Benson for having the good sense to bring me to Savannah in the first place. Her bar, the Friends Lounge, became the setting for The Lady Chablis's coronation as the Grand Empress. This is where it all kicked in for me. I put all the holiday specials together, like in 1987, when The Lady Chablis presented, "A White Christmas—Blacks Welcome." That helped launch my political direction, too—if they hadn't already been paying attention to my monologues. That's right, honey. As much as I hate to toot my own horn, please don't expect any humility from y'mama at this point in her story, 'cause y'should know that ain't the way The Doll does business.

I moved in with Bobby Ray at 416 East Liberty Street, where she had herself a condo-townhouse sort of thing. Bobby Ray Benson. She was a big sissy, and everybody knew it. We called her Helen Trouble. *Miss* Helen Trouble, baby. The first year and half or so, she was truly wonderful to me, so sweet—all three-hundred pounds of her. Stood 'bout six foot two, wore nothing but Hawaiian muumuus, Dingo boots, and drove a 1969 Lincoln. She'd drive round town and everybody recognized her in that

Continental convertible whether the top was up or down, 'cause she always had on all kinds of big ol' ugly, gaudy necklaces and rings. Oooh, she was some kinda sight—a dead ringer for the late Mama Cass in heat.

Have to give it to her, though—she was definitely a gay-community leader, specially in Savannah. She was from money and she knew lotsa politicians—y'know, had herself some connections, being that she was ol' southern stock—and so open 'bout her sexuality. Y'couldn't help but respect her. Hell, I was some kinda glad to be working for somebody who was *in there*. It would only help my own career, or so I was led to believe.

When AIDS first hit, she was the one who took up the cause for public awareness: threw them big fund-raisers and made sure her bar was stocked with free condoms. The way it is in Savannah, see, is that once y'do something good for the town, the word spreads quick to the right folks, child. That's just how Miss Bobby Ray was.

Like I said, she gave me the golden opportunity to become the Grand Empress, and all sortsa folks were coming to me after the show and inviting me to their homes, I became so popular. I was flawless. *Fuck* being Miss Gay World and all those other titles.

But don't get me wrong. I've always cherished my titles, including the one I'd picked up just before I'd left Bill McDougal's place. While I'd also been Miss Dixieland and Miss Chez Cabaret, I actually went back to Atlanta then just so I could snag the Miss Peachtree State 1985 title away from what was laughin'ly considered the competition—contestants for a Gravy Train commercial.

It'd been time for me to go back to Atlanta and let everybody know I was still around. My attitude was, yes, folks, the last time y'saw me I was a candidate for the Betty Ford Clinic, but look at me now. I'm back better than ever, and y'bitches who'd ever doubted The Doll are now cordially invited to kiss her sweet, *white* ass! Fuck y'all, 'cause I'm taking my title and heading home to Leesburg.

But first I had to win that contest.

The categories for the Miss Peachtree State Pageant included evening gowns, talent, and sportswear. I wore the same dress that

I'd worn the year I'd won Miss Gay World, but I had it re*vamped,* baby, and this black velvet Mae West number now sported a matching hat with feathers and a big rhinestone on the crown. I wore the hat cocked to one side—real sultry looking. Every time I turned round, all's y'saw was a bit of my butt and all these feathers shooting out the back of my hat. It was a hoot. Every other girl was wearing beaded dresses y'buy off the rack at J C Penney, but I went in for simplicity and elegance. It worked!

For my talent portion, I performed Patti LaBelle's "Little Girl," a song about a child coming into her womanhood and giving herself to a man for the first time. Yes, honey, The Doll had *studied* that turf. I took the whole stage and fixed it up like a playroom, with big blocks that said A-B-C, X-Y-Z, and 1-2-3, stuffed animals as big as I could find 'em, and an oversized rocking chair like li'l Miss Edith Ann's. I came out in an off-the-shoulder gown of pink satin and had on a li'l pearl necklace, my hair was pulled back into a ponytail and entwined with ribbons all the way down my back. I carried a Raggedy Ann doll and kept my gestures like that of a li'l girl, real shy, as I sang from my chair. Then, when there was an instrumental break in the song, I'd get up and walk on over to a big ol' jack-in-the-box, tap it once or twice, and one of my friends who was hiding inside would pop out. Y'bet I put my emphasis on props and staging. I wasn't coming back to a city I hated just to be left in the prayer line! No, baby, this was The Doll's second coming. Her talent portion was what won her the title.

At the Friends Lounge now, a new and improved Chablis stalked the stage, and a different circle of friends followed. Jesse McCabe became a loyal fan and customer. He also became my foundation in Savannah.

When I met Jesse in 1986, he had to have been 'bout twenty years old, but he matured with me as a gay man, as funny as that might seem. I watched him grow up from a shy and awkward li'l fag into a confident adult. Jesse never hid the fact that he was gay. He just never told his folks. They lived on the outskirts, sixteen miles outta Savannah, so he had all of downtown to be free. At times, Jesse was a li'l obvious in his gayness, had them swishing gestures he'd make with his hands, and sometimes the way he crossed his legs at the ankle made him look like he was sitting up at a Colonial Dames meeting. He was also one of those folks who everybody liked, specially after y'heard him laugh—a deep and sincere bellow that suggested his appreciation for looking at life with a giggle.

Jesse showed me Savannah and introduced me round. He became my best friend, somebody I could let my guard down in front of as I shared the evils of my past—which I was keeping real cool 'bout, since I was having myself a career rebirth that I didn't want the lid blown off of. With Jesse I could let myself go. I didn't have to constantly look beautiful, 'cause he loved me unconditionally—a situation I wasn't exactly used to, since my insecurities usually ruled, and I'd always thought my sole appeal was my stage persona.

Oh, that li'l gay boy had me. I'd never met anybody like Jesse—even in Atlanta. More than Shawn or any other sissy companion in my life, this one *sent me.*

We never did anything, y'know, *sexual.*

Sure, The Doll's tasted a li'l *restraint* in her life—on more than a couple occasions. Hmmm…make that a *single* occasion, 'cause this here was it. But I was nonetheless grateful for Jesse's laughter and friendship.

The following year, 1987, I'd discovered a new assortment of friends to clientele with, a group who didn't take kindly to illegal activities. Discriminating, y'might say they were, and some pretty tough critics, too. Officially, we called ourselves the Savannah League of Uptown White Women. That's right, girlfriend, the S.L.U.W.W. for those in the know, and those who wannabe.

The Savannah League of Uptown White Women started when me, Jesse, and this other friend of ours named Danny useta hang together on a regular basis. They knew how to cook as good as me, so we'd gather informally and have li'l dinner parties that we'd invite different friends over to each week. Some of 'em started coming back on a regular basis, so I suggested that we give ourselves a li'l name. Since I was the President and Social Director, of sorts, the S.L.U.W.W. was baptized in the name of my stage persona—the part where I pretend I'm a Palm Beach socialite, a kinda stunningly tanned example of the *Uptown White Woman.*

The members, nearly ten of us in all, were mostly gay boys and the occasional showgirl.

We usually met on Wednesday or Thursday evening, depending on whichever was Jesse's night off from Garibaldi's restaurant. One of us would call the others to say there'd be a P.T.A. meeting on such and such a night. (The P.T.A. stood for *party, talk, and alcohol*.) That was the primary function of the S.L.U.W.W.—sit round and drink and gossip, gossip, gossip, child. Anybody who breathed the air of Savannah was a target of our meetings, as we polished off my fried chicken, Jesse's chili, and Danny's lemon chiffon pie and whatever potluck surprises accompanied the arrival of our other members. Then we'd resume the cocktail hour.

ST. PATRICK'S DAY in Savannah is a twenty-four-hour cocktail party. On one grim, rainy St. Patrick's Day, Friends was packed, as all bars are on this holiday in Savannah, where one of the nation's largest celebrations is staged every year. Well, the Friends Lounge had a patio, and we'd gotten a lesbian singer to entertain some of the women outside. That way, we could do a separate drag show inside, onstage. The lezzies were all having themselves a good ol' time, but they got kinda loud, and Miss Bobby Ray was ready for 'em to leave, 'cause she wanted to let the overflow of cabaret customers spill out to the patio. So doesn't she go off on the lesbians!

"Get outta my motherfuckin' club, every last one o' you dykes," Miss Bobby Ray shouted from the same microphone she pulled away from that singer's lips.

The dykes threw their beers at her, yelled back some obscenities, and took off. Sistuh was so fucked up, she just sat down on that patio and stared at the back side of the bar for close to three hours, wearing her lime-green-and-yellow muumuu and looking some kinda stupid with her hair and face all speckled in green glitter. And there was The Doll, innocently lip-synching to Anita Baker and looking gorgeous at it, but now left to entertain a male audience that was boycotting Miss Helen's lesbian bigotry by departing in droves. I stopped my number, came down from the stage, headed to the bar, and ordered a tall sloe gin fizz. The show was over.

"We want you to come and work for us," said Burt, the owner of the Pickup, who called me the next day after word spread through town that the Friends Lounge was no longer. He was making a fortune off the gay folks of Savannah now that his joint was the only game in town.

While I was still living in Atlanta, before I'd ever met Miss Bobby Ray Benson, I'd done bookings at the Pickup. This joint was nothing new for me. In fact, a large part of my friction with its owner, Burt, was his perception that I owed him something, that if I was gonna be performing my drag in Savannah full-time, it shoulda been at *his* club, not Miss Bobby Ray's. However, ol' Burt wasn't offering me the spotlight—not then and not even now—which Miss Bobby Ray *did*, if only for a time. Burt also never learned The Doll's golden rule, honey: 'less y'speaking to her with one hand on y'heart and the other on y'wallet, she's likely to give y'the deep six!

It's gone now, but the Pickup sat there on the corner of Bay and Abercorn streets for some fourteen years. It had a very disco-seventies style to its interior: black lights and strobe lights, black walls, and that silver streaming tinsel all across the bar—the same kind y'see hanging round the perimeters of used-car lots. It was an S&M club. (That's "stand and model," girlfriend.) The Pickup attracted all of them poo-poo-pee-do young'uns, the pretty children that gotta go out and buy something new to wear every weekend and gotta make sure they're wearing enough *gourmet* Dippity-Do to keep their look in place. These were the S&M queens, who largely created the club's atmosphere, 'cause it was a huge ol' place with lotsa music and lotsa room to dance and lotsa room to cruise. Yeah, y'could go hide in the corner and grab someone's candy and nobody'd know the difference.

Another thing 'bout the Pickup's patrons, from what I observed, was a kinda bizarre but unintended tribute to the irony of gay life. For some unknown reason, what wasn't S&M clientele was usually diesel territory. And the dykes *loved* her Ladyship. I wasn't the Grand Empress for nothing, and these sistuhs made sure of that! They was the first in line to tip me and last to buy my nightcaps.

After my performance one night, this li'l blonde thang walked

YOUR FAIR LADY

on over to my barstool and handed me a single yellow rose. She introduced herself as Debbie Van Horn. Tough but tender, she was wearing a T-shirt and blue jeans. Her dry hands made me think she did lotsa gardening, and her walk was brisk, like she'd just hopped off a tractor and was fixing to tackle another chore. *A Future Farmer of America, perhaps!* I thanked her for the flower, and she mentioned something about another li'l present she had for me....

"Why, Miss Debbie, thank you so *very* much."

TOM-

FOOLERY

CHAPTER 9

CHILD, MY STORY gets complicated right 'bout here.

I lost a job and a living arrangement with Bobby Ray Benson, so I got stuck living with two lesbians, who had the only room I could find on such short notice. Dyke number one turned out to be a nasty bitch by the name of Sharon Butterfield, and dyke number two was her just-as-ugly girlfriend, Kay. While I was only renting a room in the big ol' house they shared along Crawford Square, I never felt like I had much run of the place. The only time The Doll minds the notion of guest privileges is when she's being hosted aboard a yacht. Otherwise, she's used to going and coming as she pleases.

Well, after four months Sharon started getting on my nerves, and I was some kinda PMSing. Aside from her minding my business, her and Kay constantly had those lesbian kinda arguments— the likes of "YOU LEFT THE FUCKIN' CAP OFF THE TOOTHPASTE!!!" By now, I was getting real ol' with this situation. They musta been, too, 'cause I went outta town on a booking to Columbia, South Carolina, and then on to Roanoke, Virginia, for three or four days, and when I got back to our house, there was a big-ass U-Haul out front, backed up to the front door.

Sharon and Kay said they'd found a better deal crosstown and that they'd turn the lease over to me if I wanted it. So now I've got a huge empty house, no roommates, and on toppa that, things at the Pickup were kinda shaky. Burt was already trying to renege on the salary he promised me for two nights-a-week work. He wasn't used to paying girls what I demanded in fees. Most of the entertainment he employed before me was getting fifteen to twenty bucks a show; and some of those girls was working for free just to break into the biz. Fuck that shit. We'd made a deal. Besides which, I was titled. I wasn't wearing a crown so I could be screwed royally.

But what could I do? Kick Burt's ass, knowing that he used to be a police officer and still knew the entire force, only to get my own rear end impounded? Do I quit and go homeless? Or do I keep my black, outspoken ass out of a sling and just stay put? Oh this hoogie had me, baby. By the balls. All of them bar owners always had me by the balls. That was their specialty. And as much as I tried to keep *my* balls hidden, them sonofabitches always found 'em!

Depression from all of this domestic and professional mess set in real bad, and I began boo-hooin' hard for The Doll. Soon enough, as the Lady's luck'd have it, Savannah Gas & Electric came and turned the lights off in my apartment. So now I got no electricity, no roommates, and I barely got a job....Oh, why'd I ever stop going to church?

1989 was just round the corner. I agreed to meet Miss Debbie Van Horn and my friends John and Thomas from Atlanta at the Pickup for New Year's Eve, where I'd have to perform in our biggest show of the year. After I finished my act, I went downstairs to the disco to meet up with all of them. Well, I'm standing there looking about, trying to locate their missing asses when I see this white man coming toward me with a black leather coat on down to his ankles and, under that, a black leather jacket and black leather pants. This guy's looking like a cross between Bruce Willis and Brad Pitt, and he's coming in my direction. *Damn*, I thought, *this child def'nitely ain't from round these parts!*

"Would you like to dance?" he asked as he stopped just close enough for me to get a whiff of the créme de menthe on his breath.

Like I was gonna say no? We danced all night, stopping only momentarily for me to tell Miss Debbie, John, and Thomas to go on without me 'cause I was gonna be *detained* for a while.

Mr. Man was the sexiest dancer, had everybody's attention with his combination Latin and New York disco-dancing skills. I didn't know one step. But I didn't need to. I just followed his lead and my instincts, which told me that this man wasn't working it for nothing, girl. He was fixing to show off his agility, so I'd know what was in store. Y'mama knows a smooth operator when she sees one, and she lets 'em have their way every time! And this fella had *moves:* coming up on me and rubbing his chest against mine, pecking me on the cheek just before he'd send me off in a twirl, dipping me back like I was double-jointed. Oooh, child, the crowd round us had to step outta the way. I felt like Miss Pee-Wee again, the way I once monopolized the Fox Trot dance floor in Tallahassee. We danced till my high heels was hemorrhaging. So we sat down and gave somebody else a turn.

I was in hog heaven. He had a smile about him that just drove me crazy. It went down like he was frowning, and it made me tingle every time he laughed. He happened to be in Savannah visiting his gran'parents, though his own folks still lived in Augusta, where he was from. He'd just gotten here from L.A., however, so he wasn't gonna see his gran'parents till the next morning, which left us with some time to kill. Oooh, I was gonna like 1989!

Afterward, he took me home and saw me to my door.

"How 'bout a nightcap?" I asked. He winked. I told him I lived on the third floor. He shrugged his shoulders, and in a second's swoop, this man lifted me up in his arms and toted me up three flights to my apartment door.

Once inside, he came over and unzipped my black satin dress. It was one of my stage dresses that Miss Dawn DuPree'd designed me, but I'd kept it on all night 'cause I was entitled to look glamorous for my public. As that dress slid off my slight frame, I prayed to God Almighty, *Oooh, I hope my gaff's on straight.*

Now I stood there in my panty hose, girl, and he picked me up again in his arms. I stared into his dark eyes that perfectly matched the roots of his dirty-blond hair. I lifted one arm from his neck just long enough to point to the bedroom. En route, I resumed nursing on his right earlobe like I was Miss Florence Nightingale and he was my toy soldier. He threw me onto the bed and kissed me from head to toe—sucked every single one of my toes and gently licked every square inch of my smooth ebony terrain. Honey, he really wanted to smell it!

He made *love* to me, child. I cried as my legs hugged his shoulders and he delicately ingested my titties. The smell of his head intoxicated The Doll into oblivion. Never mind the weather, girl—the steam on my windows now surely wasn't frost.

Where the hell 've y'been all my life?

The next morning, we woke up in an embrace. He gave me

that sad smile, looked past me at the clock radio, and jumped up.

"Shit, I gotta get over to my grandparents' house before they start wondering where I've gone to." I called him a cab and gave him my phone number.

"I'll be back later, sweetie," he said, giving me a light kiss on the cheek.

"I'll have y'supper ready," I said slyly. "By the way, *what the hell's y'name?*"

Three weeks later, the sonofabitch calls me from L.A.

"Who?" I asked, startled at first by his call.

"Tom. *Remember?* Baby, I can't get you off my mind."

"Really? Y'done managed for three weeks. Not that I was countin'." No, ma'am. Not likely. Even if it was really three weeks, two days, seven hours, and forty-three minutes.

Oooh, y'bet, The Doll was testy. I'd sat by that phone for a week before I'd finally told myself it was nothing more than a fantasy come to life. *Go for the beautiful moment that it was, Chablis, and don't be reading nothing else into it!*

Then he called again the next day.

"I'm going to come back to Savannah, Chablis. I'm moving in with my grandparents for a while."

Oh, is that so?

He called me 'bout every other day from that day on, but he'd never tell me exactly when he was coming. Well, a couple weeks later, Jesse and me are at the Pickup, partying on a night I had off, when I looked over at the bar from the booth we was occupying and there stood Tom, who hadn't spotted me yet.

"Oh my God, Jesse, there's my Bruce Willis!" I said, pointing but ducking down at the same time. "Right there!" Girlfriend, I was as white as Miss David Duke herself.

"Shit, Chablis! You weren't kidding!" Jesse said.

I had never been this weak for a man in all my life. I'd stood up strong to the others, but Tom left me weak and vulnerable. I'd only known two kinds of love: the powerful, physical lust I'd often mistaken for the real thing and the platonic but real love that I'd developed with friends like Shawn, Jesse, and Miss Debbie. Tom seemed like a bridge between the two, but a li'l voice inside kept warning me to rethink it, to reconsider this man. I didn't *really* know him, didn't know what was up with his work, and as much as I loved our sex together, I just didn't know if I could trust him.

Tom talked a lot 'bout his mama and his childhood, which seemed interesting to me—*prob'ly 'cause I was getting it.* He'd been living in L.A. for the last two years, but he was a country boy at heart who'd left home at a very early age for the urban life, which accounted for his leather wardrobe. When I met him, I could tell that he was streetwise, which also kinda reminded me of myself. We were a perfect fit.

I was starting to feel a li'l like a Mafia princess—The Lady Chianti. He was constantly giving me stuff—gifts, like negligees and charm bracelets, flowers and *money.* But deep down, I also knew that he hadn't poured me all the T.

Then, on one of his trips to Atlanta, Tom got stopped by the police. Apparently, there'd been a warrant out for his arrest— something to do with tickets and a traffic violation. There was also a probation violation from California, which he'd fled from in his move to Savannah. He'd already been on parole in L.A., where he was now wanted as a fugitive. So when they caught him on traffic charges in Atlanta, he also got nabbed for whatever it was they thought he did in Los Angeles, and they threw his ass in jail for three months. Don't ask, child. I didn't.

I ain't a Rhodes scholar, but I knew he wasn't being straight with me, even as my female intuition told me that he'd never deceive me on purpose. I mean, he wasn't out to con me. If anything, he kept me secluded from his shady dealings. Still, there was no denying he cared for me. From his cell, the letters just poured forth, and so did his phone calls. I was getting letters from him twice a week, and he called collect the same amount. My bills were enormous, but so was my hunger for this man.

I had time to think this relationship through while he was locked up and outta the line of my vulnerability. I knew he was scheduled for release soon, but I didn't wanna face him again. I went outta town to Valdosta on a booking when he made his way back to Savannah. I told Jesse, who had a key to my place, not to let Tom in if he showed up in the meantime.

When I got back, there was Tom standing in my apartment, the very one that contained all his gifts and his entire leather wardrobe. He was shirtless when I walked in that door—those pecs on him glistening with sweat beads, like he'd just been out running. I don't think I even wasted a moment on a greeting.

Two weeks later, Tom left one afternoon for Atlanta. He *said* he was gonna take care of things with his probation officer. He'd also said he'd be back in three days. But, child, I never saw or heard from him ever again.

I don't think I ever told Jesse, but Miss Debbie knew. I kept telling Jesse that he was back in L.A. and that I didn't give a shit if he returned or not. But everybody was asking me where he was, so I played it off to the folks at the Pickup just to salvage my pride. Besides, I had other things to think 'bout, like fixing to become a permanent piece of Savannah's history, thanks to a certain writer visiting from New York.

Jesse gets the credit for tipping me off about John Berendt. While John was living in Savannah, he was a regular at Garibaldi's restaurant, where Jesse worked. Jesse pointed him out to me one night and told me he was in town to write a book. Then and there, The Doll made up her mind to get herself into that book. As luck would have it, a few days later I was leaving Dr. Myra Bishop's office after getting my estrogen shots, and I spotted John parking his beat-up Grand Prix. I coyly asked for a ride home. John was the perfect northern gentleman, and he had no earthly idea about y'mama's T until we were halfway to my house and I told him my original name was Frank. He got all flustered and said, "So you're really a man!" In answer to which The Doll said, "Don't you be callin' me no man," and without wasting a moment, bared one of her perfectly shaped titties to prove the point. John nearly ran a red light.

But he was fascinated by The Doll, and he started coming to watch me do my show. I made him laugh. One night when he was in the audience I was in a testy mood, so I did my dance and lip synch and left the stage without doing a monologue. Later John told me I had disappointed my fans by doing that. "They come to see you talk," he said. "That's what makes you special. The dresses and the dancing are okay, but your mouth is what's made you popular. You shouldn't let them down." I hadn't realized until then that shootin' off my mouth had become my leading attraction. I've never let the fans down since then. No, honey. Bad mood or good, The Doll speaks her mind up on that stage.

One day John came to me all delighted 'cause he'd just been invited to the cotillion that the classy black folks throw. It seemed obvious to me who his date was gonna be. The way I figured it, the debutante ball was also gonna be *my* entrance in black society, baby, an opportunity to see if The Doll could really pull it off. It hadn't been too often that I got a chance to do an all-black event, so who better than the uptown socialites of Savannah to test my skills on? It was also a chance for me to go back to my roots, girl, since nearly all the people I knew or worked with in Savannah were white.

But John did not see it that way. He said, "Chablis, you must be out of your mind." No way was he gonna take The Doll to the debutante ball as his date. But by now you know The Doll. And you know The Doll would see John's refusal as a challenge. What The Doll did at the ball has become *LEGEND*! Read the chapter in *Midnight* called "Black Minuet," and you'll find out what it was. Needless to say, The Doll showed up at the ball.

I wasn't looking to create no scandal, now. I just wanted to convey some respectability and get a couple phone numbers. The Alpha Ball was also gonna be like going home for my high school reunion and getting to strut it, honey. That was more or less my attitude. But honestly, the ball turned out to be nothing more than a fancy church social. That's how I felt, with a lotta the older blacks there and the way they were dressed, with them big hats and all—y'know, how black folks *dress up* for church! I was the only one sparkling. The debutantes themselves wore simple white gowns, but not a damn one of 'em knew a thing 'bout accessorizing. So, yeah, The Doll stood out. She always does when everybody else's dress code calls for dowdy.

Maybe it was the sight of all of them black folks at the ball, but I found myself missing my family. I hadn't been home in several years. Soon enough, though, we was all planning to gather to celebrate Gran'mama's birthday. I took a weekend off from the club and headed back to Quincy. The party for Gran'mama was the first time I'd known my family to get together and do something like this. It was held at Mama's new house, the one my brother Jerome bought her with all of his *late* daddy's money. They'd invited my eighty-six-year-old stepdaddy and both Gran'mama's sisters, Aunt Mae and Aunt Gertrude. All Gran'mama's gran'children and their children were present, and all my aunts and my cousins. It was obvious from the way all the men's tongues were wagging that The Doll's extended family didn't even recognize her.

"My name's no longer Edward or Benjamin. It's Brenda! But y'can also call me Chablis," I carefully corrected cousins who only remembered me as a child. Aunt Ella Mae didn't even know who I was—thought I was my cousin Keith's date. But I *had* changed. I had myself a new name and some new titties. Wouldn't my life have been just complete if only I'd had a new man to go with 'em both!

COLUMBIAN

GOLD

CHAPTER 10

My beloved Jesse McCabe was pressing a move to Columbia, South Carolina. Needed a change of pace, he said, 'cause he felt like Savannah was getting too small. After my final walkout on Burt at the Pickup, I couldn't have agreed more. Not that Columbia's a helluva lot bigger. But it is the state capital, and it's also a university town, so, girl, y'can imagine the kinda curriculum I had planned for some of them college boys I'd be calling neighbor. I figured their diplomas wouldn't be worth shit till they'd enrolled in The Doll 101, a class that specilizes in her very own *Three Rs:* romance, rhythm, and *reservations.*

'Course, I could only offer this class on a semiregular basis, 'cause I'd really been lured to town with full-time employment at a brand-new spot called the Ménage. It was owned by the sweetest man named Keith Pyrtle. He asked me to relocate, much the same as Miss Bobby Ray had when I first got bamboozled into moving to Savannah. But Keith was different: his employees always came before he did, so I knew this time I had nothing to lose.

Jesse and me started fresh when we moved into the River Bend Apartments. We went and picked out all this new furniture—a peach-and-teal sofa-and-chair set that kinda had that Santa Fe look so popular in the mid-eighties, even though we were pushing the interior-design statute of limitations, since it was now 1990.

When Miss Dawn DuPree moved back to Atlanta from Savannah, she didn't find it any more profitable there neither. The drag bars were closing, and it wasn't as glamorous as it had once been for me, so the very talented Miss Dawn—who does a flawless Barbra Streisand impersonation—wasn't doing much of anything. I suggested that she make the move to Columbia, too. I assured her that I'd talk Keith Pyrtle into giving her a regular gig at the Ménage. We couldn't afford *not* to hire her, as far as I was concerned. She started choreographing production numbers and making our gowns the day she reported to work, so it was a professional coup that gave drag performances at Ménage the edge over other clubs in the South. And, best of all, Miss Dawn moved into the apartment above ours.

The Ménage lineup began with me welcoming the audience to the club, then doing my bit of comedy, and serving as the emcee throughout. I'd first bring out Miss Dawn, who'd come on with some more of the glamour that marks a Lady Chablis production, then Leslie the La-La Girl and Jamie the Party Girl #1 would follow. Miss Dawn also helped me write up the shows beforehand, and she'd assist me with the order of the performances, making sure that while I was onstage announcing, the other girls were backstage with their wigs sprayed and their gaffs pulled up. Mostly, Dawn and me shared the same intuition about the art of drag, playing off the strength of one another's skills without the usual cathouse bitching that makes the scene. For the first time in my career, I was headlining *and* actually producing an entire three-hour drag revue. A big responsibility? Hell, yeah, but I had all of Keith Pyrtle's faith that I could do a first-class job. So I did.

The Ménage was open for 'bout three years, when a new club called the Playground opened to great fanfare—and largely to put Keith Pyrtle outta business, 'cause he wasn't sleazy like most gay-bar owners and he wanted nothing to do with any of 'em. The Playground was our only competition, and they shut our doors with their elaborate technical sound-system and DJs from Atlanta. They didn't have much regard for drag, and they certainly didn't care much for The Doll. She was just a mouthpiece for Keith Pyrtle—the li'l nigger who talked too damn much, as far as they was concerned. But three months after the Ménage closed up, and with no other gay bars in sight, where else was she s'pposed to party?

We'd waited for almost ten minutes along the black velvet ropes that led to the entrance of the Playground when Lew Lanzetta, one of the owners, gestured to Jeff the bouncer to send us through without a cover charge. Well, just as I got to the threshold, Jeff sorta poked me with his palm.

"Chablis, we need to see your membership card," he said.

"The owner's standin' right over there and he just motioned

for us all to come in," I said, sorta puzzled since four of my *white* friends had just sailed through without having to present *their* birth certificates.

"Hang it up, bitch. You're *not* coming in here." He sorta dismissed me with a condescending laugh.

"You'll have to put me out with the trash," I said. "'Cause I ain't movin' till you gimme an explanation!" At that, he got up from his stool and grabbed me by the front of my dress and threw me against the wall.

"Bitch, you're getting outta here. Now!" And when he said that for no apparent reason other than a racist one, I instinctively took my fingernails and clawed his face till I drew enough blood to match the color of my menstrual-red nail polish.

"Miss Thing, don't you touch me!" I said, but he took my hand and twisted it behind my back, holding me in a body clamp I couldn't get out of. I was gonna be damned before I ever let anybody just beat me up. So I slid down past his knees and twirled real fast to unlock myself from him. When we stood face-to-face again, I stilettoed him in the shins with one high-heeled foot and used my nails to carve my initials in his face as he buckled over to feel his throbbing leg. Folks was cheering and concerned for y'mama from inside the club and out, where the line to get in was wrapped round the corner of the building. There was Jeff and me, blocking the entrance with our battling: I'm in my dress but kicking ass, and he's taller than me by what seems to be a foot, but I'm scratching away at his pockmarked face, while he attempts to spin me into another vice grip that my wiry li'l frame just wouldn't allow.

"Cocksucker, I ain't through with you!" I said as I took his cheap, heavy necklaces and threw 'em in the bushes. While he watched his jewelry go flying toward the shrubs, I jumped on his back, like I was ready for a game of chicken, and started pounding his head with my high-heel shoe. I was still smacking him when the club's security came and pulled me off him.

"This ain't no woman," said Jeff, whose face bore the distinct imprint of my four-inch disco heels. "She's a *he!*"

"She's a he?" the cops asked in disbelief.

"Yeah," piped up one of the other owners, who'd made his

way through the throngs of patrons to get to the scene of the crime. This guy just happened to be a retired officer himself. "Take *him* to jail!" He motioned disgustedly to the cops after taking one look at Jeff's bloody puss. I looked round for a moment, 'cause I wasn't sure 'bout who they meant.

Back for another visit to the big house.

They set the bail at $250. I decided my revenge on the Playground folks would be reserved for my court appearance. So when I was in that jail cell with all them men, I said, *Chablis, girl, y'better give that judge the performance of y'life; y'better be a comedienne or a seductress or whatever y'gotta be, 'cause this is it; jail ain't the place for a showgirl to be headlining.* After all was said and done, I think I deserved any one of Miss Susan Lucci's fifteen Emmy nominations for what I was about to do.

"The next case is number fourteen, The Playground Associates Corporation versus Benjamin Knox. Would the plaintiffs and the defendant please approach the bench?" Jeff and that former-cop bar owner moved forward. Then I stood up—along with Jesse and Miss Debbie—and approached the judge, who was, as only my Lord would have it, a woman. She was in her fifties and even kinda stylish, if you're impressed with a good dye-job and some eye shadow.

"Which one of you is Benjamin Knox?" she asked in our direction, a li'l curious as to why us three folks all came forward as the defendant. That was part of my plan, see: I wanted to maximize the shock value when she put my name to my face.

"*I am, Y'Honor,*" I said, batting my lashes and looking extraordinarily beautiful, forcing her to casually trip over pronouns. Oooh, everything was right on target.

"H-ow-w d'*you* plead, M-mmi-is-t…Knox?" She seemed totally flustered, just as I'd hoped. I didn't wanna enter a plea 'cause I was still looking for legal representation, so I asked for a "continuance," which she then granted me right away. I'd already called round and gotten the information together, child, so I knew what to say. The court changed the date for a week later, and when I returned, I came with a lawyer.

"Your Honor, we'd like to ask permission for more time to investigate the circumstances," said my attorney. He was young and white, even kinda cute in a wholesome, strawberry-blond way. But nobody I'd ever wanna lay up with.

Another continuance granted.

We went back the third time with our case totally prepared for Miss Truth-and-Justice to do her thing. I got dressed to the hilt, in a scarlet suit that looked like something Miss Diahann Carroll wore on *Dynasty*. My milquetoast lawyer wore a dark blue suit with black wing-tip shoes. Jesse was in his best threads, and Miss Debbie wore a suit. Hell, we looked like the Colbys!

The lady judge asked Jeff the bouncer to head for her chambers, where they had what seemed like a seven-minute meeting. When she came out, she invited me back for the same.

"He's willing to drop the assault charges if you reimburse him for the stitches he had at the hospital," she said in her very calm manner.

I interrupted and told her, No way; he'd started the physical *assault*. The Doll was merely defending herself against a mad rapist. Hell, if somebody provokes me, I'm gonna fight back. Wouldn't she, I asked the judge? Besides, how much damage could a li'l thing like me do to a big ol' bouncer like Jeff anyway? Wasn't he exagerrating just a bit, considering he started the shit to begin with? This wasn't about assault, it was about bigotry.

She nodded in agreement, rose from her chair, and called Jeff back into her chambers.

"Are you going to stand there and tell me this little girl right here supposedly fought with you?" she asked him very pointedly.

"Yes, ma'am." Then he paused to locate a descriptive for The Doll. "She did. *He did.*"

"I don't think this little girl could have fought with you, sir. You're six foot two, according to this personal information I have from the police report. How tall are you, Brenda, I mean, *Benjamin? That is your legal name, after all.* And what do you weigh, dear?"

"Five foot five and a half and I weigh close to a hundred and fifteen, *and I'm a size three*," I replied softly, flipping the subtle curls of my Jane Seymour wiglet to the back of my shoulders so I could fully reveal my facial expression of anger and torment.

"Now, then, we can either take care of this right here in my chambers or we can take it out there and let your lawyers try the case, but as far as I am concerned, there is no case to be tried," she said sternly, glaring at Jeff and chalking one more up to a sistuh's notion of solidarity. We exited her chambers for a quick recess with our lawyers to arrive at some consensus.

"They are willing to drop this case against you entirely. What is it that you want from them?" The lady judge asked me when we reconvened.

"Yes, Y'Honor, I'd like to see the charges dropped, but I'd also like to recover my legal fees, my bail money—even though I'm gettin' it back from the court, I want the same figure from them, just on principle—and most of all, Y'Honor, I'd like a big ol' fat apology."

"I see. Well, they've simply requested that you never return to their club again under any circumstances."

"Now, why would *I* wanna go back to their club, Y'Honor? I'll be *damned* if they gonna ever get any o' my money, child. That's no problem. Besides, it won't be there much longer anyway." She smiled.

As far as being compensated for damages? Well, I got a li'l Norma Rae in me, so I'd get back my bail money from the court, anyway. The case was dismissed. And that was the end of that.

During the time the Playground put the Ménage outta business, I wasn't working a whole lot and I wasn't booking much more neither. Thank the good Lord for Miss Debbie. She was still living in Savannah, but she was sending me cards every other day, telling me she loved me, 'cause she knew how depresssed I was. And then she'd enclose like two hundred dollars every month, for me to pay my phone bill. She became my life support: she was even driving across the border from Georgia to South Carolina just to take me to the grocery store once a week. She did that for months.

I was going through all of this brush with poverty *and* dealing with the sudden loss of Jesse, who'd one day "fallen in love" and up and went to Florida on me. It was too much for The Doll to bear, honey. I began questioning whether I had the mental stamina to endure a life on the stage, since drag ain't exactly got the universal legitimacy it deserves. My odds of being one of them supergirls seemed like a million to one at times. And I wasn't in

Savannah no more. I was living in Columbia—the Grand Empress of *Scrapin' to Get By*.

Then one day, outta the blue, I got a call from Keith Pyrtle, almost two years after the Ménage had closed.

"Chablis, I'm openin' a new bar, and before I sign any papers I gotta know if you'll come back and work for me full-time. I can't do this unless I got you."

"Keith, y'got me. When do we open?"

"We start advertisin' it as soon as I hang up the phone."

"*Bye.*"

Later that night, I went by the new club, an old movie theater, and sure enough the big marquee outside said

OPENING SOON: MATRIX
YEAH, BITCH, THE LADY CHABLIS SAYS IT'S TRUE!

Now, *Midnight in the Garden of Good and Evil* was in the process of being published by the fall of 1993. John Berendt called regularly with the progress reports, predicting early that something good might happen to me once the world got a chance to meet The Doll up close. Well, honey, it'd been so long since I'd seen him in Savannah, that, frankly, I'd forgotten that he was fixing to put y'mama on the best-sellers list. In the meanwhile, I was sorta tending to my own garden, fixing, as I was, to become a woman of independent means.

Now, I done told y'that Miss Debbie had supported me through a financial dry spell of almost two years after the Ménage had closed. I still was coming down to Savannah at least once a month to do my bookings, 'cause the Empress herself still reigned supreme, even if she did it from her throne in South Carolina. However, the money I was making wasn't nearly enough to keep The Doll in bugle beads. And the Matrix turned out to be another fizzle for poor Miss Keith Pyrtle. But three months after the year-long stint of Matrix, a new club called the Edge opened up, and before long I was back on top again.

The Edge was the most fabulous nightspot of my career, and I gotta say, they paid me damn good money for my four nights of work each week. After a three-year roller-coaster of only sometime employment, I had a hit gig on my hands. Again. I no longer felt like box-office poison. No, girl, this gay man's movie star did a li'l career rebirthing again, just like Miss Joan Crawford once done in *Whatever Happened to Baby Chablis?*

I was trying to find a new place to live, and everybody at the club knew it, 'cause y'mama was advertising it in her routines. See, after Jesse moved, I bounced round to a few different spots for the year I had that Matrix job. One night after my show at the Edge, a fan mentioned that there was a small house on a quiet dead-end street for rent, like four doors down from him, and the landlord didn't want much for it. So without wasting a second, I got up the next day, immediately jumped on my bicycle and rode on over to look at it: very small, a saltbox, they called it, with an ample living room y'stepped through a single door to get to, and a tiny hallway off of which was the two bedrooms, the bathroom, and the kitchen. Perfect.

What's really interesting to me is that this place ended up being my home for so long. I mean, I didn't have no roommates, which helped, but it marked the longest I stayed in one spot in I don't know how many years. I've still got it. Seriously, this li'l white *saltbox* was my haven of independence, a hideaway, of sorts, but mostly, a home. *My* home. At last.

Soon after I found this sweet li'l house, more good news arrived: Miss Debbie'd be joining up with me in Columbia, after the comedy club she managed decided to open a spot here.

I began spending more time with Miss Debbie Van Horn, whose knack for kindness never ceased to amaze me. She was gentle and tender and tough and nasty as any folks was capable of being. Whatever the chemistry, Miss Debbie became my confidante. She also became my roadie. The demand for The Lady Chablis was picking up at a swift pace. It was all 'bout me. In Roanoke. In Memphis. In Charleston. In Knoxville. In New Orleans. The Lady Chablis was coming to town! And there was Miss Debbie, carrying her bags!

Her and me was in the middle of giving our relationship some serious consideration. Miss Debbie gave me everything I'd needed, 'cept sex, but damn, I could get *that* anywhere, and often did. I loved it when she held me and when she wrote me her special love letters—two or three of the simplest lines of confidence-building that'd surely give Miss Dale Carnegie a run for her seminar fees. Every note she sent had hearts and kisses all over it. And I loved it whenever she and I were out in public and folks looked at us like we was two lesbians.

Well, one night, I'd finished up my booking in Savannah and drank my last kamikaze when Miss Debbie ushered me out to the car, carrying my wardrobe and whispering that she wanted us to catch the sunrise together on Tybee Island, which is just outside of Savannah by some ten miles. Said she needed to discuss something with me.

"Girl, whatever y'gotta tell me better be good, 'cause we didn't bring enough champagne to warm these beautiful bones o' mine. And this blanket ain't cuttin' it neither," I said, making it perfectly clear to Miss Debbie, as the wind slapped my face.

"I've been thinkin' about our future," she said.

"Yeah? What's wrong with it? Hell, what's *right* with it?"

"Everything's right with it." And she petted my cheek with the back of her palm. "I've gotta surprise for you, Chablis!"

So I sat up some. In front of me was a tree from the past Christmas season that the city of Savannah had brought to the shore for recycling. Now, I ain't no environmentalist, so don't be asking me what dead Christmas trees was doing at the beach in the name of ecology. But there they were, and Miss Debbie had fetched one for a li'l early morning atmosphere. She musta spent the entire night combing the sands for washed-up seashells to use as ornaments while The Doll was in town performing at the Club One. It looked like I was having Christmas at Sea World.

"What the fuck's the tree for?" I asked her.

"Mood," she said.

"*Mood?* As in, drivin' The Doll to a cold beach at four in the mornin' to look at *used* trees and ol' seashells puts her in some kinda ferocious *mood?*"

"Will you marry me, Chablis?"

"*Huh?*" She pulled out a half-carat pear-shaped diamond in a 14-karat gold setting and moved it toward my hand.

"Lemme see that ring!" I held it to the bursting sunrise and it was the most wonderful gift I'd ever known. *My engagement ring!*

I thought. A girl waits her whole life for one of these! Then Miss Debbie gently pulled it from my inspecting forefingers and placed it on the one where it belonged.

Girl, I said *yes* to Miss Debbie's proposal right then and there. She was offering me the kinda security blanket I hadn't felt in a very long time. With Miss Debbie, I could one day picture us up in rocking chairs on a porch, looking back on our years together. After all, Miss Debbie is some kinda beautiful person, and for the rest of my life I'd have this person beside me, unconditionally, who'd love me when I woke up in the morning looking like Cruella de Vil, and who'd lemme go outta the house all *incognegro*. She had the qualities that y'look for in most men and never find.

We didn't plan any wedding details right away. And we certainly didn't get registered for pots and pans at Williams-Sonoma. We just never pressed the details, child. The thing we felt most was that we wanted to do this. Logistics would be another story, baby. Everybody knew Miss Debbie was my boyfriend, fast on her way to becoming my new husband. So there was nothing to hide. I was proudly wearing a ring that I'd show to the world and would gladly tell 'em who it came from. But we first had to ask ourselves some serious questions: What were our friends gonna say? Did we give a shit? What 'bout y'folks, Miss Debbie? Y'daddy endearingly calls me *Lady Champagne,* but would he want me for a daughter-in-law? Should we give a fuck? I know Gran'-mama loves you, and I know that nothing would secretly tickle her more than if she'd found her gran'child fixing to be *groomed*. But she ain't gonna live forever, now, and neither are we.

There were also some other issues to confront. Like the part where I'd have to admit to being a big ol' *man*—y'know, for the sake of legality. Yeah, Miss Debbie, we gotta deal with society and their rules! Did I wanna put myself through that? I mean, the women of America once liberated themselves by burning their bras, baby. Was I s'pposed to do the same sorta thing now with my gaff? Well, I was willing to do that for her. For us, really.

Sure, I'd spent my adult life hiding my candy, but this was like the first time that being a *man* might actually pay off, 'least till the justice of the peace was finished with his ministering. Not that I *wasn't* planning on a gown of white lace with a long train and a virgin's veil to match. Uh-uh, girl, I surely wasn't gonna miss out on any of that! I'd only have to be a man *on paper,* in front of the county clerk who'd issue the marriage license. Who the hell would care what I wore to pick that up? I wasn't gonna let none of this traumatize me! Lord, this was the most flattering occasion of my life.

But I also had to give a li'l thought to the flip side of my answer, 'cause I knew *some* physical expression would have to be a part of it sometime down the road: Miss Debbie was pressing for us to have a child. That made brilliant sense to me, bitch. I wanted a child, too. And, God, what a gorgeous creature it'd be, right? I mean, any of The Doll's offspring would have more than a designer label on their genes! Miss Debbie had all the qualities of a real daddy—why, she even knew how to fix a car! And I had the qualities of a decent mama: the li'l shit'd make the best-dressed list! Hell, don't forget that I'd raised young'uns already, so there was no question in my mind that we could do it. But how? Would we get artificially inseminated? Or would we be navigating the copulation course with my virgin vessel?

Then I weighed some of the other deciding factors: Chablis, y'haven't got a dependable enough career that can s'pport a kid, that y'can send a kid to college with, that can buy her the Pampers she'll need all the time. Sure, girl, maybe y'can swing it for six months or a year, but what 'bout when the next club closes and y'leaning on friends again to pull y'through till someplace else opens? What are y'gonna do then? Should Miss Debbie be left with the burden of s'pporting all three of you? *And what if y'give Miss Debbie septuplets?*

Though we still remain engaged today, I don't know now if the marriage will ever happen, but I do know that I continue to love Miss Debbie more than anybody else in my life, and that she'll always be there feeling the same for me. Besides, I ain't *never* giving back that diamond!

IN SEPTEMBER 1993, John sent me an advance copy of *Midnight in the Garden of Good and Evil* as soon as it rolled off the presses. This riveting read took the literary world by storm, which is to say, The Doll musta been behind all of that thunder, baby. But after I read it, I must admit I was a li'l shocked. After all, I'd spent my entire life trying to hide my candy, and this man had done told the entire world my T! He had *exposed* y'mama, child.

Naturally, John wanted to know what I thought. So I mentioned my apprehensions 'bout having let the candy outta the gaff, if y'know what I mean.

"Chablis, you've been parading around in public as a drag queen for ten years. Everybody knows who you are already, and they love you. The book won't change anything except, possibly, make you better known."

"I guess y'got a point there," I said.

"You don't have anything to be ashamed of. You'd be surprised how many people who've read the manuscript tell me you're their favorite character. They see you as bright, quick-witted, outrageous, and enormously likable. And when the book comes out, all you have to do is keep on doing what you've been doing all along." I felt so reassured.

Next thing I know, I get a phone call from the folks at *Good Morning America*, saying they wanna do a segment on John's book and they wanna shoot my show in Savannah as part of it. So I called John immediately.

"Chablis, can you imagine all the people who'll see you on GMA?"

Hell, I thought, maybe *Oprah* watches.

"I'll do it!" I told him. Now all's I had to do was make certain I was dressed to *thrill* for my network television debut.

"Miss Dawn, girl, crank up the sewin' machine 'cause I'm fixin' to shout, 'GOOD MORNIN', AMERICA!'" Then I packed a bag, loaded my Ford Escort with a full tank of gas, and flew onto the South Carolina interstate heading yonder for Quincy, Florida. I was gonna tell Gran'mama first that the book'd finally been published—y'know, before everybody else in my life started getting up in my face. Or hers. I'd told Gran'mama years ago that I'd met a writer from New York and all of that, but we never spoke 'bout it again till now. Then I showed her every article that'd been written about The Doll's sudden celebrity and told her how ner-

vous I was that GMA was gonna come down to my weekend show in Savannah to tape me for a broadcast. Yeah, baby, she was some kinda overjoyed, hugged me till I almost choked, told me over and over how she always knew something good was gonna happen to me.

Next stop, New York—at John's graciously kind invitation. He met me at LaGuardia Airport and took me straight to Times Square, and there I was: *Lady Chablis, the Musical.* I found myself smack dab in the heart of Manhattan, which I hadn't seen since I was twelve years old and up there at the Harlem Institute of Fashion, sewing myself some capri pants. The February streets were filled with slush and winos, and the icy sidewalks made *strolling* a li'l difficult. But The Doll knew cold, child. So she smartly brought her leather coat, her leather gloves, her scarves, her boots, and her *furs.* She had her suits and oversized coats. She was prepared, girlfriend, and her seven suitcases attested to this.

That night we went to dinner at this fancy restaurant. The place was white-woman headquarters for the fabulously privileged and those who think they are. As we were led to our table by this handsome maître-d' with broad shoulders and a Cary Grant jawline, we got stopped by a buncha blue-haired uptown ladies. The blue-haired kind is the most uptown y'can get, so naturally I was captivated by the fact that they recognized John from his book-jacket photo. Then he introduced me, and, girl, I felt like I'd been asked to join the Junior League!

"Pick up *USA Today*," John called to say 'bout a month later. I opened it to the Life section, and I remembered that, only just a couple of days before, Oprah Winfrey'd said on her show that she always read the Life section of *USA Today* first, 'cause that's what told her everything she needed to know 'bout entertainment. And so I was keeping that in mind as I opened to the Life section's front page, and all's you saw was this picture of The Doll engaged in her favorite pastime. No, child, not that one! I mean, The Doll in a red gown, looking at herself in the mirror and doing her hair. The caption read, "The Garden Grows," and the first line went, "The Lady Chablis is preparing." Yeah, bitch, she's *preparing* to run for president, but y'all can read 'bout that in her sequel!

THE REAL

McCOY

EPILOGUE

AT-TEN-SHUN! (AT THE NATIONAL GUARD, SAVANNAH)

IF Y'SEE MY life as I do, y'realize it's been one big metaphor for that journey to the human state of being known as respect.

If y'think being gay is tough, try being a transie! Professionally speaking, drag has served as an obvious pursuit for a girl like me. Where else could I enjoy the limelight in an evening gown? It's a career that's allowed me to earn a good living while being *entirely* who and what I believe myself to be at the same time. The downside—and there's always one of those—is that drag has often been a life led in platinum handcuffs. See, this profession hasn't yet achieved the understanding and respectability that it deserves as an art form—*La Cage Aux Folles* and all of that mess aside— and that might enable its growth to broader audiences and outta the exploitive and sleazy clutches of most gay-bar owners.

There is, however, an exception to every rule. And I've known two of 'em in my career: Keith Pyrtle, the boss I moved to Columbia, South Carolina, to work for in 1989, and a white woman by the name of Miss Joan McCoy, who's passed on, but who, more than any other person, I'll always remember. She'd first seen my show in Atlanta at the Locker Room, fell in love with me, then called and asked to book me. And so began a professional association at both of her gay bars and a personal relationship the likes of which I'm sure I'll never know again. Miss Joan was one of the few anchors I've ever known, and if I didn't mention her sooner in my story, it's 'cause I've saved the best for last. She touched my life in such a way that a day doesn't go by that I don't carry the essence of her soul with me.

Oh, the bitch intimidated the hell outta me.

She had to have been damn near sixty-three years old when I met her. Big ol' diesel dyke. Tough as nails. Oh, she'd seen the gay revolution, honey, lived every second of it in its purple battlefields and wore those scars like a decorated soldier—a veteran lezzie who carried herself like a woman to be reckoned with. Very proud and dignified. Polite but very assertive. Her stride was long, and her arms stayed stationary when she moved. She was totally in control of herself. Her posture had a rigid and almost masculine air to it, but there was something of a work of grace inscribed in the way she held her head—tilted, as if her pointed nose caught every smell that entered its vicinity—and by the way she kept her mouth so solemnly shut till she spoke. And when she did, those were gonna be some direct sentences, to the point. Clipped even. Not 'cause she didn't know lotsa big words—she did—she just wasn't gonna waste them if she didn't have to.

No, she wasn't formally educated, but that was a technicality, really, 'cause Miss Joan knew about subjects like art and politics and history way beyond what y'can glean from reading the newspaper. For a girl like me who never finished high school, I considered every moment spent with Miss Joan to be my college years. She taught me more 'bout culture than any ol' boring thing I've ever watched on PBS. Not that she ever had to prove nothing to nobody, 'cause she didn't care what folks thought. That's what came across the minute you met her, the minute her big blue eyes pierced and assessed you like she was taking inventory in the liquor cellar of one of her bars.

She always carried a gun, a small Smith & Wesson pistol with a mother-of-pearl grip that she kept in the left breast pocket of the blazers that were her uniform. I'd asked her once why she needed one at all.

"Just to sober up the poor clown who mistakes me for some damsel in distress," she'd said in her typically cynical way, just as she'd offer up the tiny half-smile that was her own admission to possessing a sense of humor, which she had in abundance but, like everything else she valued, used sparin'ly.

Na-a-ah, Miss Joan had no use for men in general, felt they were no damn good. Not 'cause she was a lezzie. She just thought most of 'em were lazy bastards who used the privilege of being male to disguise what they didn't know or couldn't do. Oh, she caught 'em in the eye on that one. Ironic'ly, though, men seemed to be the whole reason she existed the way she did: independent of 'em in a business world in which she also thrived alongside of 'em. I never knew why she was a man hater, 'cause she was not fundamentally opposed to men, say, in relation to a woman like me. What she loved most was to take me to the local joints where there was a bunch of Bubbas gathered round talking and fuck with their heads by telling 'em what I was.

"Betcha haven't seen a girl as pretty my lady," she'd joke to a buncha hoogies she sensed were making lesbian cracks at her expense.

"No, ma'am. She's quite a looker," they'd often return just as they'd ask the bartender to send us a round.

"Betcha'd never know that this pretty li'l thing is actually a *guy*," she'd press on. This would make 'em quake every time. Miss Joan'd really delight in their reactions as they sorta scattered away, 'cause it was her way of getting the last laugh on 'em while proving her point that most men were as dumb as they looked.

Illness started taking a toll on her own looks in the eight years I knew her. She was nearly bald from a disease called lupus, so she wore a variety of wigs from Eva Gabor's line, 'cept that all of 'em were short and all of 'em were blonde. Funny, she favored the frosted shag most, the one that made her look like Mrs. Carol Brady, and yet she didn't go in much for fem'nine indulgences none. No, ma'am. She wore custom-made men's-style suits, but in a way that didn't look like drag, 'cause they hugged her five-foot-six frame and gave her average weight some of that hour-glass flattery. Everything she owned was conservatively tailored in darker colors and finished with a silk scarf worn like an ascot, which added a li'l contrast to the starched formality of her white—*and always white*—blouses. This was her costume, her uniform. I never saw her in a pair of jeans or anything else for that matter. She'd be *dressed*, baby, in a way that few women can approach even in their finest. I guess this is what's known as *real* style.

Miss Joan was already a millionairess by the age of thirty. She collected every penny and played the stock market with the same intensity a bookie does horses. A businesswoman, she owned the Take-Two Lounge, a lesbian bar; the Fast Lane, a black gay bar;

plus another club, for a straight clientele. All of 'em in Augusta, where she lived. She was sixteen when she left home to flee the intolerance of her folks, who wasn't gonna stomach the fact that their daughter wasn't no debutante. She told me once she'd saved every nickel she got working odd jobs as a bartender, enough so she could put a down payment on an ailing saloon, which she turned round—by turning it lesbian—in no time flat. One lezzie bar led to another. Hell, she'd prob'ly sold off four of 'em before she came into my life in the early 1980s, when I was still Miss Gay World.

What I loved most was to listen to her talk.

"This painting, Lady, was actually done in Montana in the 1930s. There's a distinct possibility that this artist studied with Georgia O'Keefe...," and how Miss Joan would go on. But it gave her pleasure to share what she knew with me, 'cause for her, that was the same as confiding in a friend. I mean, most folks consider other folks friends if they can dish out the dirt and share confidences, but she didn't go in for any of that. She didn't waste time with small-talk exchanges, so when she shared her passion for art with me, that was like an invitation to her inner sanctum. Somebody snotty mighta dismissed me as a stupid li'l nigger, but Miss Joan was the first person since that cherubic Miss Monroe, my fifth-grade teacher at Stevens Elementary School, who gave me a chance when it came to learning.

On toppa that, I was her number-one showgirl. Before anybody else got a booking, she'd ask what dates on the calendar I wanted. I could always pick up the phone and tell her when I needed some work. As far as the other girls were concerned, everybody knew how tight me and Miss Joan was. We was the best of buddies. Even Rita, her companion, didn't try to interfere. What Miss Joan and me had comes once in a lifetime, girl. Be jealous if y'wanted to, but it was a waste of your time.

I remember when I was having my red-hot love affair with Miss Crystal Meth and I was about to be thrown out on the street. It was Miss Joan who came to my rescue.

"Give me every bill you've got," she demanded, just before she pulled out her checkbook and paid every one of 'em.

Then she sat down and prayed with me. We talked and we

prayed. She picked up her Bible and begged the Lord not to turn His back on me. She even invoked a passage from First Corinthians 9:22: *"To the weak became I as weak, that I might gain the weak: I am made all things to all men, that I might by all means save some."* But Miss Joan didn't ever do much *advising*, so to speak. She was a true s'pporter, which is harder to find since just 'bout anybody'll hand you advice. Most of all, she taught me what dignity meant.

Miss Joan had to fight for what was hers in a world that didn't take to kindly to a woman, *a lesbian*, who was financially and emotionally independent of men—'specially in the South. She saw in me the same struggles toward self-worth and acceptance that she'd endured to get to where she was. Personal honor was hardwon by Miss Joan. Nobody ever mentored her, so she saw to it that I received the kinda survivalist coaching she never had.

She did lemme have it one time during the course of our friendship. It was the only time Miss Joan and I ever had it out.

I was coming from Atlanta to do a show at Miss Joan's bar. It was me and this sexy lesbian, Chrissy Hancock. Bitch was beautiful: blonde curly hair down her back and titties like y'see in a centerfold, so firm and round, her nipples the size of half-dollars, and the rest of her body was just as blessedly molded. She did shows—lip-synching and some light grooving to the music—much like a drag queen does, only for female audiences.

First of all, we got there late—like it was midnight when we arrived—and it was all the fault of my tardy ass, so Miss Joan was already pissed. Chrissy went on and the crowd went up for her, yelling and screaming, as she sang "Angel of the Morning" sitting on a chair backward, and kicking it away just as the song came to its climax ending. They loved her, sure, but it was nothing I didn't think I could top.

I went on. Light applause. Strictly courtesy. No hollering and no hooting. *Wait a minute.* I hesitated some, which threw me off my stage rhythm, my ability to stride and sashay like I was used to—outta the curtain to the thundering sound of a full house clapping all at once and drowning the musical number with their cheers. So I fizzled fast and never regained my mood or my momentum.

"Damn y'all, sonofabitches," I yelled after Miss Minnie Riperton's "Lovin' You" phased out in its high-pitched *lalalalala*-ing squeal. The audience hissed. "*Fuck* y'all!" I couldn't believe they were treating *me*—The Lady Chablis!—like this for some damn *tuna tartare*, y'know?

Well, Miss Joan appeared right there on stage, pulled the microphone from my grip, and led me off, while them dykes down below continued to boo The Doll.

"How dare them dykes throw me to the *side* for that woman, Miss Joan?"

"Chablis, these customers are *lesbians*. They are into women. You are *not* a real woman. You've got to understand: they can't go home and fantasize about you!"

"But this here's *my* club!" Well, I got a tendency to get possessive sometimes, but this here wasn't gonna be one of 'em. Miss Joan sure reminded me of that when she *slapped* me back to Earth.

"No, Chablis, this club belongs to *me!*" She was some kinda pissed that I'd take advantage like that.

I was so sorry.

Well, Miss Joan didn't try and punish me or keep me outta her bar again, but she did make me think about my priorities as a performer—that the amount of applause had li'l to do with the quality of my performance—that each audience would be different, so my expectations were always gonna be best if they were reserved for me.

MISS JOAN LOVED her reefer. It was the only thing that helped ease the pain of her lupus, which'd made her skin swell up and ate at her bones, causing them to ache constantly. I never knew how much pain she was in till the end, when she had to stop coming to my shows 'cause the loud music and the bright, dizzying flicker of the strobe lights would make her head hurt and her body ache even more.

She'd call me at all times of the day. Sometimes four or five o'clock in the morning. Anybody else call me at that damn hour woulda done lost their mind—*and a few other things once I got through with 'em*—but Miss Joan just wanted to talk. So I'd turn on the light, fluff up my pillows, light me a cigarette, and just listen. She'd have to hang up first, 'cause I was gonna make sure I was there as long as she needed me for, and I was *always* gonna make sure I made her laugh before the conversation ended.

The next morning she'd call back.

"I'm feeling better today, Chablis. Thanks for listening to me last night."

I hope that gave her some strength. She was fading fast.

One night, musta been in mid-1989, she called me just as I was packing what few things I was gonna take with me to Columbia.

"Chablis, I can't take this pain anymore. I've got to do *something*." I lit a cigarette and settled in.

She told me how important I was in her life. Even more so than her relationship with Rita, who was kinda like a roommate and business partner more than anything else. Then Miss Joan asked me to go get a passport, 'cause she wanted me to go to Italy with her. Just the two of us. She was a world-class traveler. That was prob'ly the only thing besides her art that she spared no expense for. Italy was where she'd educated herself about history and culture, where she'd traveled the countryside many times over the years to taste the foods of each region. She felt connected to that country somehow, even though she was Irish. She wanted to die there, surrounded by all the things that ever really mattered to her. And she was gonna kill herself. She wanted me to be there with her when she took her life.

"Would you please go with me? I know it's a lot to ask, but I love you and I trust you, and I need you to do this for me."

God, forgive my sin, but I just couldn't do it. Oh, Miss Joan, I hope you're reading this in heaven, girl, 'cause as selfish as it seemed of me then, I loved y'too much to witness your exit from this world. But she was by herself when she took an overdose at her home in Augusta to put an end to her disease. And I've never regretted anything so much—that I wouldn't keep her company in the last hours of her life, once she'd determined the pain was too great to go on.

Oh, God, I regret it—that eats at me all the time. I wake up many mornings with knots in my smooth li'l gut, haunted by what a selfish bitch I was not to grant Miss Joan her last wish. She never once asked me for anything, and the one favor she needed most—*one final favor*—I just couldn't give her. I'd reconciled that Miss Joan wasn't gonna live forever. I knew that. I just wasn't emotionally equipped enough to deal with the gravity of her request. She'll always be alive in my heart, but when the angels came down to take her soul, I just didn't wanna watch.

Rita, who'd prob'ly exchanged a dozen words with me in the course of my friendship with Miss Joan, called me the very next day with the news of her companion's suicide.

"Chablis, Joan did it." That's how she told me over the phone. "All by herself. I just found her." I didn't say nothing back, so Rita sorta just hung up. I stood there holding the phone, completely unable to move. It was as though I'd had a premonition and seen it come true. Oh, I sure coulda used some Psychic Friends at that moment. I was numb, baby. I felt as though a part of me had died with Miss Joan. I couldn't even cry 'cause I was too busy hyperventilating from the devastation of what Rita'd just told me.

Only a month before Miss Joan died, I'd been taking a few bookings a month at another club in Augusta called Trixie's. This way I could earn a paycheck and look in on Miss Joan regularly. Well, one night, after I finished emceeing the Miss Gorgeous Georgia Pageant, Brucie, the owner of this club, came to me with a request.

"Chablis, we wanna give Joan McCoy an award."

"F'*what*? The bitch-a-lot award?" I said jokin'ly.

"No, because she's been so good to the gay community."

And she was. She was always flying to New York to bring back ideas for her clubs—whether it was suggestions for contests and theme nights or musical trends like break dancing and imported dance tracks from Europe or any kinda political awareness in the age of AIDS—y'know, anything new and different so that the kids in Augusta could learn. Miss Joan was all for learning.

"I wanna give her an award," Brucie continued. "And I wanna call it the Joan McCoy Humanitarian Award. We'll pick somebody who's done something for the community each year and give them this award in her honor. Will you present it to her?"

Miss Joan met this news with her typical modesty.

"These folks wanna give y'an award," I told her brightly. She was really sick at his point and more or less confined to her bed. "I'll get 'em to bring the award to y'personally, Miss Joan."

But, no, she got up, threw that "Brady Bunch" wig on toppa her head, put on a blue pinstripe suit and an emerald scarf, and limped up to the stage that night with her cane, in sheer agony, just to have the pleasure of receiving that award from me. She leaned her cane against the podium and made a grab for her Chablis. She held me so tight, I could barely hand her the framed certificate.

Later, she asked why they hadn't waited until she was dead. Strangely, it was only a week later that she was. But y'could tell from the way she faced the audience and waved a couple times, as if she were trying to silence their applause, that the entire evening and that humanitarian award was one of the proudest moments of her life.

A few weeks after Miss Joan's death, when I'd had a chance to collect myself, I called and asked Rita for that award. I'd never had much to say to the woman in the past, but she knew what Miss Joan and me meant to one another. Yeah, sure, Rita said, and quickly mentioned giving it to me as soon as she found it, but I never heard back from her again.

Miss Joan mighta left me some money, but more importantly, she left me one *flawless* memory. She was the one who taught me to be proud of who and what I am. She really helped me see that. That ol' bald-headed bitch, she did that. She wasn't close to a lotta folks, but she loved her sistuh Chablis.

More than anybody else in my life, Miss Joan made me realize that I was worth something. She gave me the kind of mothering—y'know, the grown-up kind that's more 'bout being equals than one having it over the other—that I still needed to become a full-fledged adult. I was her family, the daughter she never had.

"We don't go there, Chablis," she responded once to my question about her own family's whereabouts. I never asked again. Ironic'ly, though, when my daddy died in 1984, she was the one who forced me to return to Quincy for his funeral.

"Of course, you're going, Chablis!" insisted Miss Joan. "He's your father, no matter what." Then she handed me two hundred dollars to buy a black dress and rent a car. And, y'know, despite the b.s. with my daddy's sisters, I'm glad I did, 'cause when I got there and saw his grave in Quincy's black-folks cemetery, it put closure on a lotta things that had bothered me 'bout him during my growing up. Y'know, I was his only child, and there'll be no more Knoxes, 'cause I've already begun my menopause, so I ain't gonna be birthing no babies! I knew he was hurt that I was never gonna carry on the family name, but that's the way it was, and that's the way it is.

Back then, I was still too young to see what the hell Miss Joan was talking about, but now I do. See, dignity only counts when somebody else can see it. And Miss Joan knew that. She always knew.

Miss Joan, girl, thank you so much for everything you ever did for me. Y'gave me a sense of hope and destiny, and y'taught me that I control both. I make the rules, just like you did, Miss Joan. Sure, I look back on my career and know that I ain't gonna be up under them lights lip-synching to Anita Baker forever and traveling back 'n' forth between Columbia and Savannah or wherever the compass points of my next gigs happen to be. Who knows? I'm a talented comedienne, so there's always my dream of doing stand-up, maybe for *Girls Night Out* on Lifetime Television for Women, if they're listening up. And I'm a writer, too. Y'just know I got a sequel or two planned. Acting? Honey, I do that every time I gotta go outta the house for milk and eggs.

Seriously speaking, I think 'bout a lotta the gifts I've been given. I got myself a steady whose name I ain't gonna reveal, 'cause I've told y'enough already. There's Miss Debbie, still hoping we'll take the plunge. I got Gran'mama still and all my other relatives in Quincy who I speak to. Mama and me sure done put aside the past and forged ourselves a nice future. My health— well, knock wood 'cause it's still there, too. I tell myself that if I ever had to face any grave illnesses—and, let's face it, a girl who's been on the scene of gay life as long as I have, bitch, has got to— I guess I don't really wanna know. Don't need to. When the Lord says it's time, there's no negotiating. And I'm looking forward someday to one kick-ass reunion with Miss Joan. I mean, she was

SOLDIER OF FORTUNE

my greatest example of how *never* to let anything overcome y'spirit, 'cause that's the Lord's turf. And so, with all the grace she showed me, I know I'd do the same. That's why I hide my candy.

Everything 'bout me otherwise is natural 'cept my titties, and as I've explained, I take pills to grow 'em. My breasts are something the Lord can forgive me for, 'cause they're not perm'nent. I reckon He's gonna ask, "Where's that *thang* I gave ya? Y'know, Benjamin Edward Knox, y'cannot come up in here if you ain't got it. I wanna see it now!"

Well, I wanna tell Him back, "Here it is, honey. It might be all shriveled up and ugly, but I got it! Now open them damn gates, Lord, and lemme in!"

THE LADY

CHABLIS

LEXICON

(THE DOLL USES HER OWN TONGUE.
THIS IS A GUIDE TO HER PERSONAL
VERNACULAR OF WORDS AND PHRASES.)

ALRIGHT, MISS THING: *[phr.]* A statement of my approval.

BUGLE BEADS: *[n.]* Long glass beads y'string onto y'gowns to make 'em sparkle.

BUSTIN' A NUT: *[v.phr.]* What y'do by y'self when y'mama ain't looking.

CALL IT OUT!: *[v.phr.]* To tell it like it is, child.

[to] **CLIENTELE:** *[v.]* To have an association with somebody in the mixing and mingling sense.

[to] **CLOCK,** and [have] **DONE CLOCKED:** *[v.]* To know what time it is when it comes to my biological gender.

[to] **COME BUSTING OVER:** *[v.]* To show up uninvited, only to have The Doll slam the door on you.

CRACK MY FACE! (or, **CRACKED!**): *[v.phr.]* To be embarrassed by something completely unexpected. *(Such as a sweet li'l child being able to clock The Doll.)*

DON'T BE GETTING UP IN MY WORLD: *[v.phr.]* Stay outta my business, my personal affairs, and my problems. *(All possessive pronouns may be substituted here.)*

DRAG DAUGHTER: *[n.]* A showgirl who's just starting out and needs some mothering.

DRAG GIRL: *[n.]* A female impersonator.

DRAG SISTER: *[n.]* A female impersonator who's also my friend.

DRAG SON: *[n.]* A young gay guy, new to the gay lifestyle, who needs advice and protection.

FISH: *[n.]* Drag-queen slang for biological females.

[the] **4 1 1:** *[n.phr.]* Information, child; what else? If there's something y'need to know, just ask The Doll and she'll give y'the 4-1-1.

GAFF: *[n.]* A cloth device that looks like a G-string that us showgirls use to conceal *it*.

GIRL, GIRLFRIEND: *[n.]* A biological girl or any person who is gay, fem'nine, or *open-minded*.

HIDING MY CANDY: *[v.phr.]* Thanks to my gaff, honey—*a way of life!*

[a] **HOOGIE:** *[n.]* Poor white trash; *a redneck motherfucker.*

INCOGNEGRO: *[adj.]* How to describe The Doll without her wigs and makeup.

IN FACE/OUTTA FACE: *[adj.phr.]* In drag/outta drag; your *face* is y'makeup.

IT'S Y'FANTASY, GIRL (or, **BABY**): *[phr.]* It's what y'think or wish or pretend could or would or did happen.

JUKE JOINT: *[n.]* Black slang for a run-down ol' club. (*My mama owned one of these when I was a kid.*)

KIDS: *[n.]* Young gay people.

LI'L DEBBIE SNACKIN' CAKE PUMPS: *[n.]*
Shoes with less than a three-and-a-half-inch heel. *(Not to be confused with* Miss *Debbie, who don't wear no pumps! Ever.)*

MISS CRYSTAL METH: *[n.]* A powdered form of speed that, once-upon-a-time, gave y'mama a *run* for her *money.*

MISS THANG: *[n.]* Me.

MISS THING: *[n.]* You.

MR. MAN: *[n.]* Fine, good-looking, and firm.

MY T (TO KNOW MY T, TO TELL MY T): *[n.]*, *[v.phr.]* Knowing where my candy's hidden; knowing that I even *have* candy.

NOT 'LESS Y'MAMA SAYS GO: *[phr.]* Not unless I give y'permission.

[to be] **ONE OF TOMORROW'S MEN:** *[adj.phr.]* A young male child with gayish or effem'nate tendencies.

PARTY FRIEND: *[n.]* A friend to socialize with only; a partner in crime in the club and bar scene.

POUR THE TEA!: *[v.phr]* Tell The Doll the truth, or *dish the dirt*!

P.T.A.: *[n.]* Party, Talk, and Alcohol; associated with the agenda of the S.L.U.W.W. *(See below.)*

PUNK: *[n.]* Black slang for sissy or gay boy.

[to] **PUT A COOKING DOWN:** *[v.phr.]* To cook a feast that entails a lotta time and a lotta love.

SERVING IT; SERVING IT ON A PLATTER:
[v.phr] "It" is beauty, and if y'strut *it* well enough to catch The Doll's eye, baby, y'earn her highest compliment.

SHOWGIRL: *[n.]* A drag queen.

SISTUH: *[n.]* Everybody's favorite sibling, *me*; but sometimes, *you*.

S.L.U.W.W.: *[n.]* [The] Savannah League of Uptown White Women; a li'l club that a couple of my friends and me started to honor the belief that all of us is entitled to spend our days sitting up under hairdryers, going to lunch, and riding round town shopping—*all at somebody else's expense.*

SMELL IT!: *[v.phr.]* To have a whiff of my perfume—a special blend of strawberry-vinegar and water. *(This phrase is the signature of The Doll.)*

[to be] **SOME KINDA———:** *[adv.phr.]* The Doll's own personal adverb.

[to] **STUDY:** *[v.]* To know of where I speak, girlfriend.

T: *[n.]* The truth.

TELL THE STORY!: *[v.phr.]* Give The Doll the dirt, child! *(When this phrase is said to closet cases, it means, Come Outta There!)*

THAT'S Y'WORLD: *[phr.]* That's y'business. *(All possessive pronouns need apply.)*

THE DOLL: *[n.]* Petite to please in a perfect size three; *that's me, baby.*

THE LADY: *[n.]* Chablis herself, of course.

24-HOUR GIRL: *[adj.phr.]* Drag queens who always appear as "girls," whether on—or—offstage.

TWO TEARS IN A BUCKET, MOTHERFUCK IT!: *[phr.]* Cry over the crisis and *go on now! (This phrase is the motto of The Doll.)*

UPTOWN WHITE WOMAN: *[n.]* The persona of a classy, extravagant, and glamorous woman—big car, big rings, etc. *(This term can be used for all women regardless of color.)*

YOU'S A BIG OL' SISSY: *[phr.]* Ain't nobody gay-er than you, child!

Y'AIN'T ALL OF THAT: *[phr.]* Not [to] be everything y'*say* you are; not [to] be everything y'*think* you are.

Y'MAMA: *[n.]* That's me, so show some respect.

Y'THE ONE GIRL!: *[phr.]* Y'the *best.*

Y'WEARING IT OUT!: *[phr.]* It's all about you, baby, and whatever it is, y'doing it *right.*

THE DOLL

DOES

DINNER

(A Home Recipe Companion of
Victuals and Fixin's.)

"THE WAY TO a man's heart is through his stomach."
Now, y'know some uptown white bitch prob'ly came up with
that theory. But the truth is, child, I've been known to lure a man
to my lair by feeding him first. 'Course I've also been known to
feed a man after he's fed me some himself.

The Doll's got many tantalizing ways of securing a man's heart,
and although a lot of 'em involve *eating and feeding,* none of 'em
involves cooking if she don't have to. Sure, I prefer to be wined
and dined, *specially if I'm PMSing.* But when the evening calls
for intimacy, y'don't wanna be sitting up in some restaurant when
y'own kitchen's only steps away from the bedroom. *You are what
y'eat, isn't that right?*

So on those occasions, The Doll covers her ass with the tried-
and-true culinary delights that've been handed down to genera-
tions of Ponder women, the very recipes for which she's kind
enough to provide y'with below.

BRENDA'S KICKIN' CHICKEN

This is real southern fried chicken. And I learned this famous
recipe at the knee of the Colonel, along with a couple other
things he showed me.

You'll need:

2 whole chickens	*pepper*
2 cups flour	*seasoning salt*
vegetable oil	*paprika*
salt	

Usually, I take two whole chickens and cut 'em up myself. Like a
Texan with a chainsaw, I slice the titties sideways, then pull off the
legs.

Then I take an ol' plastic bread or grocery bag and fill it with my seasonings: two cups flour, and y'own determination of salt, pepper, seasoning salt, and paprika to taste. Now, y'have to use a plastic bag—otherwise it'll taste just like plain ol' chicken. The plastic makes the chicken sing. It also saves my lazy ass from having to clean another bowl.

First I rinse the chicken well. *Y'don't know if it ain't been whoring in the henhouse before it wound up in y'grocer's freezer.* Then I pat it dry. *Pretend you're a dominatrix and give it a good swat!* And I always add some extra pepper while it's still raw—I mean, *moist.*

Then I place the chicken in the bag with the seasonings and give it all a good shake, rattle, 'n' roll.

I use a liquid oil—never shortening. Then I heat it all in a black cast-iron skillet. And I know it's ready when I throw my seasoning mix in and watch it sizzle, child—*the same way The Doll does on stage.*

I lay the chicken in the skillet *gently.* Not that I give a rat's ass how the chicken feels. I just don't need any scalding grease marring my transluscent skin. Then I cover the skillet and let it all cook for 15 minutes on the one side.

Then I flip 'em over for another 10. And then I take the cover off for the remaining 5. This split-timing makes the chicken moist and crusty and good and crunchy. *Yes, ma'am.*

I take it outta the skillet and place it on paper towels to let the grease drain. After that, I throw it all on a platter.

Hell, y'didn't expect garnish, too, didja?

*Now, if y'frying ass is just too lazy to make chicken at home, get on the next plane to Savannah, stop by Mrs. Wilkes' Boarding House and go to the back door and grab a bag of their takeout. Hers is the second-best fried chicken in the South.

BRENDA'S BEEFY SURPRISE

This recipe is good for feeding every man. It's simple and inexpensive. And if he complains, tell him to stick his candy in an electrical socket.

You'll need:

1½ lbs. ground beef	*1 box instant mashed*
1 onion	*potatoes*
3 stalks of celery	*2 cups of sharp cheddar*
2 cans cream of mush-	*cheese*
room soup	*salt*
1 cup milk	*pepper*
16-oz. package of	*paprika*
mixed veggies	

Preheat y'oven to 350°.

Brown the ground beef in a skillet with chopped onion and celery. Drain.

Put y'mixed veggies in a bowl with some water and heat in the microwave till tender. If you've only got a stove top, do the same procedure using a saucepan. Drain and set aside.

Prepare y'instant mashed potatoes according to the directions on the box. *I ain't gonna read it for you.*

In a big ol' bowl, combine the milk, the cans of soup, y'drained veggies and the ground beef.

Now spread this God-forsaken mixture into the bottom of a baking pan. Then add a layer of cheese, and then a layer of the mashed potatoes on top. Sprinkle with salt, pepper, and paprika to taste. And place in the oven for 30 to 45 minutes till the top is golden brown.

Then pull it out, baby, and feed the boys!

SMACK Y'MAMA'S RIBS

There ain't nothing like down-home ribs to satisfy a man's hearty appetite. Mine are so lip-licking fine, he'll be thanking y'with diamonds, girlfriend. These taste specially good after you've gotten stoned.

You'll need:

country-style cut ribs or spareribs (if y'must)
barbecue sauce (KFC's Masterpiece BBQ sauce is my personal favorite.)
1 can of Bud (Yes, child, for the marinade. Why the hell should y'be the only one partying?)
salt
pepper
seasoning salt

Preheat y'oven to 450°.

Make sure y'wash and scrub those ribs! *Y'ain't gonna sue me for salmonella poisoning!*

Place cleaned ribs in a shallow cooking pan. Season—according to taste—with salt, pepper, and seasoning salt. Now add the entire can of Bud.

Cover with aluminum foil and place in the oven for 1½ hours. *Now, don't be opening the oven to peek at it or nothing. This special preparation is gonna be tenderizing the meat and keeping the moisture in. Trust The Doll on this one, baby.*

When time's up, remove the pan from the oven and drain the fat. Now y'ready for the grill. *Or the broiler if y'live in New York City.*

Coat the ribs with y'choice of barbecue sauce and place 'em on the grill in no special order. *This ain't y'underwear drawer y'arranging.* You'll only wanna brown 'em till the sauce sticks to the ribs, 'cause the oven's already done the cooking part.

Now call the boys to the picnic table!

BRENDA'S CALLING COLLARDS

This is the same recipe I used when I entertained the Clarence boys from Chapter Three. I hope y'get the same results I did! *You'll need:*

2 bundles of the freshest collard greens y'can find
2 southern ham hocks or 2 lbs. of smoked neck bones

½ cup of sugar
2 tbsp. of vinegar
salt
pepper

Fill a six-quart pot with water and bring to a boil, adding y'meat. Now y'gonna boil that meat for 45 minutes to an hour, till it's tender and jumping off the bone.

While the meat's boiling, prepare y'fresh greens. Cut each leaf off the stalk and rinse it separately. Stack 6 to 8 leaves and roll 'em up the same way you'd do y'hair in curlers on a lonely Saturday night. Then cut the roll crosswise into small pieces. *Y'with me?*

Add the sugar and remaining ingredients to the boiling water. Now add the prepared greens, stirring briskly to shake 'em loose.

Lower heat and simmer for 1 to 1½ hours, till soft and tender.

The sugar and the vinegar remove the bitter flavoring and leave behind a taste that's kinda sweet and sour. (*Like a good kamikaze shooter!*)

BITCHIN' BISCUITS

This is my special cornbread recipe known throughout the South. It's the cheapest to make, and it'll taste the same every time.

Yes, baby, after thirty-some years of cooking, The Doll relies on Jiffy Mix. *I told y'it was known throughout the South.* Just follow the directions on the Jiffy box and take note of these li'l additions: add ¼ cup of bacon grease and a tablespoon of sugar, and y'cornbread'll come out tasting like pound cake! *Y'welcome.*

TITILLATING TATERS

This is The Doll's famous accompaniment to her fried chicken. If y'paying attention, you'll see why it's both easy and economical, and y'don't have to be a kitchen wizard to try it.

Take several large potatoes and slice 'em like french fries. Soak 'em in water for 30 minutes. This keeps 'em from discoloring to a sickly brown color. *Yes, child, even them veggies wanna be uptown white women!*

Go back to my Kickin' Chicken recipe and note the seasoning mixture; it's the same one you'll use here. *Y'gonna need another plastic bag, too. So find another place to put y'reefer.* When y'got this mixture concocted, throw in those sliced potatoes and put a shakin' down.

Now deep fry just the way I do my chicken. And drain the grease on a paper towel. When they've cooled some, throw 'em on a platter and add salt to taste.

Watch those fellas munch with gratitude.

And when they're done munching, y'can reward 'em with these taters!

PICKANINNY PUNCH

This is Aunt Tee's recipe for kick-ass punch. Use sparingly for seducing purposes, 'cause nothing functions after two cups. For those dumb enough to drink more than that: explain to them doctors in the E.R.—those ones who'll be pumping y' stomach—that y'momentary discomfort ain't fatal. Then when y'faculties have returned, please write me in care of my publisher, and I'll make sure y'lawyer's subpoena gets to Aunt Tee

You'll need:

2 to 3 bottles of ginger ale
3 big cans of pineapple juice
2 packages of lemon-lime Kool-Aid mix (with that big ol' smiling sissy on the packet)
¼ cup sugar (to help Miss Kool-Aid do her thing!)
fresh fruit slices: lemon, *lime, pineapple, cherries, peaches*—if y'know as many fruits as I do, girl, y'won't have any trouble adding to this list.
1 pint grain alcohol (Now, y'don't expect me to list the states that sell this shit, do you?)

First, take a bundt cake pan and fill with cold water just a quarter way. Now add all y'diced fruits and freeze. Then refill with water and freeze. This is gonna be y'ice mold, which you'll need later.

While this is freezing, grab y'punch bowl and stir in all the liquid ingredients—'cept for the booze—and set aside to chill.

Add the ice mold and grain alcohol only when it's party time, and not a minute before, 'cause the ice'll melt and the grain alcohol—at 190° proof—will lose its strength and conviction.

The cowardly may substitute Vodka, but their sissy asses ain't welcome at any party The Doll throws.

MAMA'S MAC 'N' CHEESE

One of the few things Mama ever done right. So good, it'll whisk y'back to Quincy.

You'll need:

two 8-oz. blocks of sharp cheddar cheese (either store-bought shredded or the slice-y'own variety that The Doll prefers)	*2 eggs*
	1 to 1½ cups milk
	1 minced onion
	2 to 3 tbsp. flour
	1 stick of butter
	salt
one 16-oz. box of maca-roni noodles	*pepper*
	paprika

Preheat y'oven to 350°.

Boil noodles till tender. Drain and set aside. Take cheese and cut into chunks, *'less y'lazy ass bought it shredded—in which case, get the fuck outta my face while I'm slicing.*

In a skillet, brown y'butter, flour, and minced onion. Lower heat and add milk, stirring to thicken.

Once it's all nice and thick, *and The Doll loves things nice and thick,* add 'bout half y'cheese.

When y'cheese has melted, add y'drained macaroni and stir some more.

Now place the noodle mixture into a casserole dish and layer with the remaining cheese, so that y'end up with a cheesy top layer. Sprinkle the top with paprika to taste.

Place the casserole into the oven for 35 to 45 minutes till the top is golden brown, but not dry.

When it's done, help y'self to a big ol' heaping, and tell *y'guests to serve themselves.*

GREAT AUNTIE CHABLIS'S ORIGINAL HOMEMADE PECAN PIE

Seeing as that bitch Betty Crocker musta done pilfered The Doll's own secret recipe for good ol'-fashioned pecan pie, may I suggest that y'trot y'ass over to y'local Barnes and Noble, head straight for the cookbook section—quietly and real crafty and coy, like y'was Agent 99—now look both ways down the aisle, as if y'was crossing the street, and discreetly pull the volume from the shelf. Okay, stop and clear y'throat as y'look round to make sure no in-your-face salesperson is lingering in y'midst, then go straight to the index. Now while y'doing this, look up and yawn, keeping one eye on the pages y'flipping till y'get to the right one. When you've located the recipe, hold y'finger in place while y'pull that hankie from y'back pocket—see, y'snotrag's gonna stifle the blow of that big ol' sneeze you'll fake in order to camouflage the sound of the page being torn from Miss Betty's cookbook. Now take the hankie and the recipe and stick 'em both back in y'pocket at the same time. Then saunter outta that store as if you've just dropped a hundred bucks on books, and when y'get to your car, drive off in the motherfucker like y'was headed to the hospital! When you've returned home without an arrest for vandalism, shoplifting, or speeding, take that recipe outta y'back pocket and paste it in the space below.

SO Y'

WANNA BE

LIKE THE

DOLL

Beauty and fashion Tips For the
Aspirin' transvestite

I'M READY FOR MY CLOSE-UP!
(IN THE DRESSING ROOM AT CLUB ONE, SAVANNAH)

Y'ALL BETTER HOPE that y'blessed with *natural* beauty like I was, 'cause all the cosmetics in the world ain't gonna make y'as beautiful as the Lord can! I'm one of the lucky ones, and I know it. Plain and simple. Now, there ain't nothing wrong with looking better, and the more natural you are with y'cosmetic *assistance,* the more natural you'll come across to others. And, let's face it, y'always want folks to like y'for y'self and nothing else, right? *Even though we all know that that's a load of crap, 'cause folks'll always judge y'by appearances.* So when the day comes that y'can walk round like me, a natural beauty, without so much as a stitch of makeup on, you'll also prob'ly be starring on Broadway, too. Stop y'dreaming, child, and listen up!

BEAUTY

✦ First rule of thumb: keep y'makeup organized and very conveniently placed. Y'just never know who might come a-knocking, so y'need to be ready. Like, say the milkman starts approaching y'door, you'll wanna throw on some lipstick right quick. So, again, as a matter of practicality above all else, keep the shit handy just in case.

Now, during my career as an entertainer and also during my reign *as a female,* I've noticed that certain types of makeup come and go, but like all good things in life y'always come back to the basics. Where makeup is concerned, we're talking black eyeliner and red lipstick. The eyeliner, drawn in the crease of the eyelids, has proven to be this girl's best friend. Nothing else sets off her most valuable feature better than a good eyeliner pencil. Mine is by Maybelline, but y'can go ahead and get ripped off by Chanel and Elizabeth Arden if y'prefer. A good eyeliner allows y'to recreate y'self depending on y'mood. Like for evening, y'might wanna Color Yourself *Barbra,* 'round 1965, and do her ol' cat's-eye look—y'know, the one that requires a matching leopard coat against a full-length mirror at Bergdorf's to really pull it off? Yeah, baby, with the money Maybelline'll save you, that air fare to Africa and the subsequent fine for leopard poaching oughta seem like a real deal.

✦ Lips. I'm a faithful believer in red lipstick. It'll always be in, and it'll always be the most seductive color. Lip-liner is a good idea, too, specially in a color that's a li'l darker than y'lipstick. This'll make y'lips protrude without the need for costly collagen implants. Natural-looking colors are okay, but realize that I'm a girl who believes in vamping, honey. Vamp, vamp, vamp! Leave all the petite, pretty stuff, honey, for the other folks. In other words, go on and be a "ho."

✦ Another beauty trick of mine includes contouring. If y'have very few facial features of any strength, a li'l contouring'll go a long way, child. Being the very tan white woman that I am, I'm apt to take a dark brown or plum, or deep earth tone and make a line underneath my cheekbones, then I smooth out the lines with a brush so that they don't look like the same scar G.I. Joe wears. The blush goes on toppa all that smoothing. Now blend it again, baby. This'll make y'cheekbones appear even higher. If y'gota big ol' wide nose, y'might wanna take a contour brush and—starting from the bridge and heading toward y'nostrils on each side—draw a sharp line that you'll smooth and blend exactly as we did with our cheeks above. This nose contouring'll help y'give the illusion of a perky LaToya nose job.

✦ I'll say here and now that there's nothing wrong with wearing false eyelashes. They can be very complimentary. A girl needs long lashes, specially us black girls, honey. While we usually make up for it with our titties and our butts, we're a li'l deficient in the hair and eye departments. So go ahead and Krazy Glue them lashes, 'cause without 'em you'll prob'ly look like a mole. Y'can buy just the top lashes or the bottom lashes, or both. And remember, too, if y'know how to put 'em on properly, y'less likely to get clocked. Use eyelash glue or hair-binding glue only. And know that there's even glue in every color to match y'own. You'll look that much

more natural with the right color glue, so don't be slathering on the Elmer's, or y'deserve to have y'T told to the rest of the world.

✦ Now, growing up, I've always had problems with my skin. Yeah, as much as I hate to admit it. And cooking fried chicken all the time and exposing myself to spitting grease don't help any. So at least three times a week I give myself a facial where I'll take a facial steamer—which I advise y'to purchase, too— and I'll steam my face with some chamomile tea for ten minutes and then apply a clay or peel-off mask, which I let sit and harden for about twenty minutes more. Then I remove the mask, and off come the particles that can stick to y'pores and make y'look all bruised and wrong and ugly and nasty, child.

Now, if y'can't find a facial steamer at the local Wal-Mart, put a pot of water and chamomile tea on the stove and bring it to a boil, then put the pot on a towel, somewhere near where y'can sit comfortably. Take another towel and put it over y'head as y'lean your face into the steam rising from the pot of just-boiled water. This is known as *pot steaming*, honey. This is a facial recipe, baby. Ain't nothing y'serve for dinner. It is, however, something y'do before being *taken to dinner*.

✦ Use lotsa hairspray to keep the shit from flying round, but don't be using the ol'-fashioned kind that makes the man in y'life feel like he's back on the football team every time he touches you and bumps into y'helmet! And keep those eyebrows nice and plucked by investing in a pair of Eckerd's or Revco's tweezers—y'know, the ones that got the angled points so they can grip those coarse hairs that refuse to be uprooted? And if there are a couple other stray hairs elsewhere on y'face, y'might wanna keep those tweezers handy. Now, I mention this 'cause I've been told that some women going through menopause grow themselves a bit of a beard; then again, there are some of us girls who grow beards without menopause. So a good pair of tweezers should follow y'round like a new puppy. In fact, y'might wanna get several pairs: throw one in y'purse, keep one in the car, one in y'desk at work, on the night table next to y'bed, in the den where y'do y'needlepoint, at y'dry cleaner's, y'grocer's freezer....

FASHION

✦ Accesorizing is numero uno on the fashion front. In my line of business, *shoes* are a very crucial component to the art of illusion. Whether y'matching 'em up with a beaded gown or a li'l black dress, y'shoes is y'stock-in-trade, and folks is always gonna be checking out y'feet to see if you're a big ol' man. But back when I couldn't afford to buy shoes reasonably priced enough so as to match every outfit I had with her own pair, I'd often go to the Goodwill or the Salvation Army or a consignment shop and look for white satin bridesmaid shoes in the five-dollar range, the kind that y'can dye y'self—at home, child, and in a rainbow of colors. If y'can dream it, you can create it—that's my color motto. If y'feel like splurging 'cause y'saved so much on the shoes, then go and have 'em professionally dyed. But y'prob'ly thinking, Shit, Chablis, ain't those shoes a li'l *unsanitary?* To which my response is, Hell, no, girl! No bridesmaid wears her shoes twice. The most she ever done did was stroll down the aisle on the arm of somebody she prob'ly didn't like and later left the reception early 'cause she didn't wanna have to give him none after a few drinks—or took 'em off to fuck him, anyway. Besides, if the dye doesn't disinfect the shoes, Lysol sure won't!

✦ Another fashion rule of thumb: y'don't have to wear clothes with a designer label to look good! Always buy according to fashion; but know that whatever's up in them magazines can be found in a thrift store or consignment shop. If y'must, look round Marshalls and Filene's Basement. There are ways of inexpensively finding the labels, and there are ways of inexpensively knocking off the labels. If y'smart, you'll opt for the latter. 'Course, personally speaking, I got my own dressmaker—Miss Dawn DuPree—so I really don't really give a shit 'bout labels—not yours or Calvin Klein's. Besides, y'mama's gotta hold on to her money, so I advise y'to do the same.

✦ Panty hose. Well, I'm a No-Nonsense girl. So I make sure to check the circulars on Sunday that advertise the two-for-one sales, then I buy as many pairs in the shades I like, or as many as I can fit in the trunk of my car. And I drive a big-ass, uptown-white-woman's Buick Park Avenue, so that's a lotta trunk space! Stock up and you'll never need nail-polish remover, 'cept, of course, for y'nails.

These are just a few tips to get y'started on the road to becoming a crowned beauty. Remember, y'ain't never gonna look as good as me, so don't despair, 'cause you'll only be wasting y'time. Do what I do to enhance my God-given beauty, and y'got a fighting chance of at least getting a date next weekend.

See y'in Hollywood.

BRENDA'S

BLUE

BOOK

THE LADY CHABLIS'S SOCIAL REGISTER:
AN INDEX OF WHO'S WHO AND WHAT'S WHAT

I'VE GOT'CHA NUMBER.
(AT THE HAMILTON TURNER MANSION, SAVANNAH)

A

the **ASHLEYS:** *Gran'mama's employers*

AUNT ELLA MAE: *One of Mama's sisters; she was the least accepting of my female development.*

AUNT GERTRUDE: *Gran'mama's sister.*

AUNT KATE, also known as **AUNT KATIE BELL:** *Mama's sister, who helped raise me till I was nine years old.*

AUNT MAE: *Gran'mama's other sister.*

AUNT PATTY: *Another one of Mama's sisters; she's cousin Keith's mother.*

AUNT TEE: *Yet another one of Mama's sisters, and an English teacher at my junior high school.*

B

BELK: *A huge department-store chain in the South; it was also the site of my first and last big jewelry heist.*

Miss **IRENE BELLE:** *If ever there was a mean-ass bitch, this woman was it; she taught me in the fourth grade at Stevens Elementary School.*

Miss **BENJI:** *A nickname for The Doll, honey, back when she was just coming into her adolescence.*

Miss **BOBBY RAY BENSON:** *The owner of the Friends Lounge in Savannah, who we also called Miss Helen Trouble.*

JOHN BERENDT: *The writer who's responsible for y'mama's sudden fame; he put her up in that best-seller of his,* Midnight in the Garden of Good and Evil, *and he did a real fine job of it, too.*

BESSIE: *My daddy's no-good bitch of a sister, who I ain't ever gonna see again.*

Dr. **MYRA BISHOP**: *My doctor in Savannah, whose prescriptive advice helped me maintain my girlishness.*

BOSCO: *My late, great cousin—and Aunt Katie Bell's only child—who taught me how to behave in public*

BRIARWOOD: *The apartment complex in Atlanta that Shawn and me moved into, where we met Miss Denise.*

BURT: *The sleazebag owner of the Pickup in Savannah, who screwed me outta my pay, only to discover he manipulated the wrong girl.*

SHARON BUTTERFIELD: *A lesbian I lived with for a short time in Savannah.*

C

Miss **CHEZ CABARET PAGEANT**: *The first title I ever won.*

the **CLARENCE** boys: *My neighbors in Quincy, who I served up my special fixin's for whenever Mama was outta the house.*

CONNIE: *A very dear soul who let me live with her in the Quincy projects during some abusive times in my youth.*

Miss **RHONDA CONYERS**: *One of the great influences in my life and a partner in crime during my teen years.*

CYNTHIA: *My second oldest half-sister.*

D

DANNY: *The li'l gay guy who introduced me to Kenny Reardon at the Locker Room in Atlanta.*

DANNY: *Another li'l gay guy; this one in Savannah and a member of the S.L.U.W.W.*

DEEDEE: *A nice bisexual li'l black girl who took The Doll home to Miami for an evening she's never forgotten.*

Miss **MELISSA DELANE**: *That powerful black bitch lawyer who got The Doll acquitted in Montgomery.*

Miss **DENISE**: *Shawn's and my neighbor and good friend at Atlanta's Briarwood apartments; she still thinks I'm a full-fledged postoperative transie!*

Miss **TINA DEVORE:** *My drag mama.*

Miss **MARY ANN DILLON:** *Quincy's number-one shoplifter, who didn't coach The Doll well enough to stay outta jail.*

The **MISS DIXIELAND PAGEANT:** *My second crowned title.*

DONNY: *A nurse and a fellow sissy who took The Doll to see Alvin Ailey perform in Tallahassee.*

DUST BUNNIES: *The li'l cleaning business I began in Atlanta before Miss Crystal Meth got the best of me.*

Miss **DAWN DUPREE:** *My seamstress and my drag sister.*

DUCHESS AND RANDY: *She's a transie; he's from Quincy; together with Kenny and me, we all shared an apartment in Atlanta.*

E

EARL: *A computer geek and my dear friend who let me hide out at his place after Kenny walked out and Duchess and Randy were getting on my nerves with all their pampering.*

the **EDGE:** *The last club I headlined at in Columbia, and my all-time favorite workplace.*

EDWARD: *My middle name at birth, and a name by which I'm still referred to by my gran'mama.*

F

DESIA MAE PONDER KNOX WHITESIDE FAIRLEY: *Mama, by any other names.*

Mr. **JOHN FAIRLEY:** *My stepdaddy.*

JOHN FAIRLEY, JR.: *My youngest half-brother.*

FAIRLEY'S DRYCLEANERS: *My stepdaddy's business in Quincy, where The Doll spent many evenings after school collecting everything but wages.*

Dr. **FEINBERG:** *He prescribed my first female hormones in Atlanta.*

the **FOX TROT:** *My first gay bar experience in Tallahassee, where I made my drag debut.*

the **FRIENDS LOUNGE:** *A cabaret bar in Savannah, where I had my first headlining job and got crowned the Grand Empress.*

G

GARIBALDI'S: *My favorite Italian restaurant in Savannah.*
The **MISS GAY WORLD PAGEANT:** *My main crowned title that I won in Atlanta, which helped to launch my fame throughout the South.*
GRAN'MAMA: *My one and only, and the greatest lady I know. [See also Miss Anna Mae Ponder.]*
SAMMY GREEN: *My second teen romance was with this guy, who sported an amazingly large box for a guy of fifteen.*

H

HARLEM INSTITUTE OF FASHION: *Where I did what I did on my summer vacation as a teen.*

I

ILLUSIONS: *A club in Atlanta where I met Shawn, Max, and the Men in Motion.*

J

JAMIE THE PARTY GIRL #1: *A drag queen, who was part of my production lineup at the Ménage in Columbia.*
JEFF: *My blond hunk of white frosting from* Midnight in the Garden of Good and Evil.
JEFF: *The prejudiced bouncer at the Playground in Columbia who made y'mama stoop to fisticuffs.*
the **JETAWAY:** *A black club in Miami, where I'd never pick up another guy again.*
JOHN AND THOMAS: *A gay couple who are as close to me as family.*

SO MUCH TO DO, SO LI'L TIME.
(HAMILTON TURNER MANSION)

K

KATRINA AND SABRINA: *A couple of prostitutes, who showed me the fine art of hooking when I first moved to Atlanta.*

KAY: *The lesbian girlfriend of Sharon Butterfield, my brief roommate in Savannah.*

KEITH: *My cousin; Aunt Patty's boy.*

BENJAMIN EDWARD KNOX: *Who I was; my legal birth name.*

BENJAMIN FRANKLIN KNOX: *My daddy.*

BRENDA DALE KNOX: *Who I became.*

L

LAVELLA: *One of the black debutantes at the Alpha Ball, and the sister of my man Philip.*

LESLIE THE LA-LA GIRL: *A drag queen, who was part of my production lineup at the Ménage in Columbia.*

LEW LANZETTA: *One of the owners of the Playground in Columbia, South Carolina.*

LILA: *My daddy's girlfriend; a Latin tamale he was dating the summer I spent visiting him in New York.*

LINDA: *My white best girlfriend and roommate in Atlanta; she was a stripper, and kept us in the lap of luxury.*

the **LOCKER ROOM:** *A club in Atlanta that hired me after I won the Miss Dixieland Pageant.*

LOIS: *My oldest half-sister; she's better known as Peachy-Pat.*

M

MAMA: *The one and only.* [See also Desia Mae Ponder Knox Whiteside Fairley]

LARRY MARKS: *My first li'l boyfriend; he taught me how to masturbate.*

MATRIX: *A short-lived club in Columbia, where I worked as a headliner for Keith Pyrtle.*

MAX: *The manager and emcee of the **Men in Motion** male-strippers revue, which I kinda usurped when they added me to the bill.*

JESSE MCCABE: *My best friend in Savannah during the years I first lived there and a fellow charter member of the S.L.U.W.W., who I had myself a deep crush on.*

Miss **JOAN MCCOY:** *The best employer and friend I've ever known.*

BILL MCDOUGAL: *The man from Leesburg who saved me from the evil clutches of Miss Crystal Meth.*

the **MÉNAGE:** *Another short-lived club of Keith Pyrtle's in Columbia, where I headlined.*

MISS MONROE: *My wonderful fifth-grade teacher and an early influence.*

the Reverend **FELIX MUNSON:** *The minister at Connie's church in Quincy, who took to confessing his sins to The Doll.*

N

JIM NALLY: *The Onyx's bigoted owner.*

O

the **ONYX:** *The club in Atlanta where it all began for me professionally.*

P

PEACHY-PAT: *My oldest half-sister Lois's nickname.*

Miss **PEE-WEE:** *My teen name in Quincy.*

PHILIP: *The boy who swept me off my feet at the Alpha Debutante Cotillion.*

the **PICKUP:** *A club in Savannah I ended up walking out of when the owner tried to stiff me.*

PIGGLY WIGGLY: *One of the South's biggest supermarket chains. Haven't y'seen Driving Miss Daisy?*

the **PLAYGROUND:** *The club in Columbia known for its racist door policy.*

Miss **ANNA MAE PONDER**: *My gran'mama and the sweetest woman who ever lived.*

PRINCE GEORGE INN: *My first non-show job in Atlanta, where I worked as a salad person and had my first adult romance with one of the waiters.*

KEITH PYRTLE: *A very good friend and employer in Columbia; he owned both the Ménage and Matrix, where I performed exclusively at each.*

Q

QUINCY: *My hometown in Florida.*

R

RANDY: *Miss Tina Devore's seventeen-year-old plaything, who lived with us when we first moved to Atlanta.* [Not to be confused with Randy of Duchess fame.]

KENNY REARDON: *One of the great loves of my life, but him and me had problems we couldn't iron out.*

the Misses **LOIS AND MARGARET REEVES**: *These two sisters got the ball rolling; they taught me how to cross-dress when I was just fourteen.*

RENEE AND CAROLYN: *These lesbians lived in my Aunt Kate's trailer park in Tallahassee; they took me to my first gay club, the Fox Trot.*

RICH'S: *Atlanta's big department store.*

RITA: *Miss Joan's companion.*

S

NICK SCOUT: *The owner of the Yum-Yum Tree in Montgomery, who was kind enough to post my bail.*

SHAWN: *My dearest friend in Atlanta during the later years there; he gave me my very first traditional Christmas.*

STEVENS ELEMENTARY SCHOOL: *My grammar school in Quincy; home of sweet Miss Monroe and that mean ol' bitch Miss Irene Belle.*

Mr. **CALVIN SHEARER:** *My junior-high school instructor in the Future Farmers of America; he was the first person to ever utter the word "homosexual" in reference to y'mama.*
BILL SULLIVAN: *The kindly Onyx bartender who helped me make my way in those early Atlanta days.*
SUSIE: *My daddy's well-meaning sister, who I only met once, at his funeral.*

T

THE LADY CHABLIS: *Ultimately, my stage name, but a bit of a phenomenon, too.*
TOM: *The man who loved me and left me in Savannah.*
CLIFF TAYLOR: *The male alter ego of Miss Tina Devore, my drag mother.*
Miss **HELEN TROUBLE:** *What we called Miss Bobby Ray Benson, owner of the Friends Lounge in Savannah.*

U

UNCLE LONNIE: *My Aunt Kate's husband and cousin Bosco's father.*

V

Miss **DEBBIE VAN HORN:** *My lesbian fiancée.*
MOHAMMED VARTANIAN: *My first romance in Atlanta was with this Middle-Eastern man.*

W

Mr. **CLYDE WATERS:** *My protector at the Quincy jail after my shoplifting debacle.*
Mr. **CHARLES WHITESIDE:** *Mama's second husband in Chicago; father of my half-brother Jerome.*
JEROME WHITESIDE: *My half-brother.*

Y

the **YUM-YUM TREE:** *A club in Montgomery, Alabama, I never got to play, on account of a li'l run-in with the local deputy.*

NOTE: SOME NAMES HAVE BEEN CHANGED TO PROTECT Y'GUILTY ASSES!

BYE, BITCHES!

A SPECIAL THANKS TO CHEVON SCOTT
[HAIR AND MAKEUP], DAWN DUPREE [FASHION], AND
ESPECIALLY THE KIND CITY OF SAVANNAH